E M O T I O N A L
I N T E L L I G E N C E
—— 3.0 ——

*May this be your
best year yet !*

Tomi Bryan

EMOTIONAL INTELLIGENCE

3.0

How to Stop Playing Small in a Really Big Universe

DR. TOMI WHITE BRYAN

HOUNDSTOOTH
PRESS

Emotional Intelligence 3.0
How to Stop Playing Small in a Really Big Universe

ISBN 978-1-5445-2938-7 Hardcover
      978-1-5445-2937-0 Paperback
      978-1-5445-2936-3 Ebook

Dedicated to Dad, Mom, and Jim.

Because it always

had to be you.

ALSO BY DR. TOMI WHITE BRYAN

(Pen Name Tomi Llama)

The 5 Keys to the Great Life

by Dr. Jerry T. White and Dr. Tomi W. Bryan

What's Your Superpower?

by Tomi Llama

The Tomi Llama Purpose Guide:
Emotional Maturity as a Path to Your Divine Purpose

by Tomi Llama

Hating Myself Every Step of The Way:
Tips and Tools for Stepping Out of Self-Hatred into Self-Love

by Tomi Llama

Contents

Section II

THE BACKDROP
OF EMOTIONAL BALANCE

SHIFTING THE FOCUS

A New Foundation: Systems Thinking

Emotional Balance

Transparency

ORGANIZING PRINCIPLES

Organizing Principle #1: System Dynamics

Organizing Principle #2: Spiral Dynamics

Organizing Principle #3: Creation Dynamics

Organizing Principle #4: Energy Dynamics

Connecting the Dots: Organizing Principles

Section III

THE NUTS AND BOLTS OF EI$^{3.0}$

THE POLES OF EMOTIONAL BALANCE

The Adapted Identity

Childhood Experiences

The Family System

Cultural Systems

The Effects of These Systemic Influences

Section IV

NEXT STEPS

THE
BETTER
CONVERSATION

Chapter One

THESE BRUISES

Here, feelings are good. Here, feelings are powerful. They are indicators of what is stirring inside each of us. Every feeling you have is important, serves a purpose, and should be embraced and honored, especially if you want to maximize your potential. I know these might be radical ideas for some of you, mainly if you grew up in an environment as I did, one where there was no crying in baseball and, when you did cry, the refrain was, "Keep it up, and I will give you something to really cry about."

As you might imagine, I have been on a long, tumultuous journey to understand my feelings so that they guide and inform who I am rather than derail me. And while my childhood was emotionally harsh, I can't imagine making the journey to this moment in any way other than working through the emotional layers of the past fifty-plus years. It has been a grand adventure, and it's not over; in some ways, the adventure is just beginning.

Like many of you, the unconscious emotional layers that limited my ability to tap into all my potential are rooted in my childhood experiences. I don't blame my parents; my parents were good people who were not in emotional balance. I followed in their footsteps and became a good person who was not in emotional balance, either. We do what we know. In a way, I am grateful to them, as my uniqueness is directly attributable to those layers. As the lyrics to the Train song "Bruises" suggest, "these bruises make for better conversation."[1] Yes, my bruises do make for better conversation—and give me a unique flavor—as do yours.

It took, and continues to take, a substantial amount of work to discover the space of emotional balance, where my feelings are guides and not guards. That's why I wrote this book—to help guide others down this path of Emotional Intelligence 3.0. Throughout my life, I have felt compelled to maximize my potential. I have come to see that every time I missed the mark, it was because I lived by an omnipresent and omnipotent unwritten rule I learned from life: *It's not safe to be who I am (so I must be something else, and the system will dictate what that is).*

My emotional experiences continually reinforced this rule in a way that led me to think these two thoughts about myself: *I am not lovable as I am* and *I am not powerful as I am.* The more my emotional experiences reinforced these thoughts, the more I believed them, and the more I behaved in accordance with them. Ultimately, an *I am not lovable as I am* emotional imprint and an *I am not powerful as I am* emotional imprint formed out of the familiar ruts and grooves I created from bumping up against the rule's limits. Encoded into each imprint was the meaning I had unknowingly assigned to the original emotional experience. It also included a habitual feeling and a rote action that honored the boundaries of the unwritten rule and maintained a *comfort zone* for my life.

Emotional imprints are either bruised or refined. The meaning, habitual feeling, and rote action associated with a bruised emotional imprint are imbalanced, hiding that you are a magical, creative ball of energy with infinite possibilities. If the imprint is bruised, the meaning assigned to the imprint is also hidden from view. These bruised imprints guard you, ensuring you remain within the *comfort zone* established by the unwritten rule. The job of this zone is to keep you from stepping outside the invisible fence created by your version of the unwritten rule. These bruised imprints are also a primary reason for low emotional intelligence and the inability to become the best version of yourself personally and professionally.

A refined imprint is one where the meaning and feeling have been processed, so the resulting action is emotionally balanced. Processing those bruises balances the imprint, so it guides you as you navigate all the possibilities that exist for your life. Once refined, you can finally see that you have always been lovable and powerful.

I will elaborate on both types of emotional imprints and the boundaries they create for our lives in later chapters. Now, though, I share the rich layers that contributed to my bruised emotional imprints, and show you how they were woven into my emotional fabric. The story begins with the emotional imprints of my parents and the bruises they each brought to their marriage.

Both of my parents had difficult childhoods in Richmond, Virginia. My father, Dr. Thomas King White, was only seven when his father passed away in 1939, leaving the family in a difficult situation. His mother, Irene, had no formal education and struggled to make ends meet.

Irene's story is complicated. She had been "traded" to my grandfather Grover at fourteen. It was, allegedly, a fair swap: Grover's sister, Alice, was supposed to marry my great-grandfather, Frank Walton, in exchange for Irene marrying Grover. Alice refused to marry Frank even though Irene married Grover. See Figure 1 for an abbreviated White Family Tree.

THE WHITE FAMILY

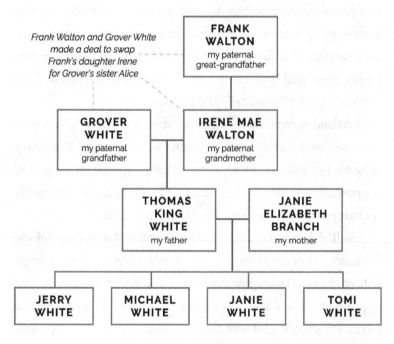

Figure 1. Abbreviated White Family Tree.

When Irene married my grandfather at age fourteen, she became a stepmother to six children. Her oldest stepchild, Annie, was fifteen. Grover and Irene had six children. One of them died in infancy, and

Irene was pregnant with her seventh when Grover died. My grandmother was now a widower with five biological children in the house and one child on the way.

One way Irene provided for her family was to become a lady of the night. I make no judgment of my grandmother's choices. I have only respect and admiration for her ability to figure out ways to maintain food and shelter for her family as best she could.

Irene subsequently gave birth to two more children by one of her longtime evening friends. Even though they were not Grover's biological children, they were given the last name White.

With so many children and no education, Irene struggled. The White family moved every few months because Irene couldn't consistently pay the rent. She couldn't always provide food, either. I can only imagine how desperate my grandmother must have felt at times. These experiences left deep psychological scars on my father that followed him his whole life. They also forged an unbreakable bond between my dad and some of his siblings.

When my dad was old enough, he went to work in the meat department of Mr. Harvey's grocery store in Richmond. Mr. Harvey was a wise, compassionate, and kind man, a much-needed father figure to young Tom White, who learned a great deal about life from him.

Still, times were tough. Irene sometimes sent one of her younger children, Charlie, to find Dad at the store when there was no food in the house. Dad would be working at the meat counter when little Charlie would peek around the corner of that counter—and Dad just knew. He silently cut a pound of bologna, wrapped it, and gave it to Charlie. Mr. Harvey took payment for that food from Dad's wages each paycheck.

When Dad joined the military, he started boxing because each bout's winner would get a ribeye steak dinner. He told us he loved eating that ribeye so much that he went 27–0 in military boxing matches just to get that steak.

After my dad left the military, he attended college and graduate school, ultimately graduating with a PhD in psychology. Shortly after graduation, we moved to Durham, North Carolina, so that Dad could teach at the University of North Carolina at Chapel Hill. The university was a short commute from our house in Durham. We included my mother, Janie; my three older siblings, Jerry, Mike, and little Janie; and me. In addition to landing a great job at a prestigious university, there were three other important reasons my father moved us to North Carolina. The first reason was that Dad needed some breathing room. As he aged, he was starting to feel suffocated by the unbreakable family bond forged in the fight for survival with his siblings. He hoped the distance between Durham, North Carolina, and Richmond, Virginia, would provide the necessary space to breathe.

The second reason we moved was my father's complicated relationship with his mother. My dad's childhood experiences with his mother became his unconscious story that you can't trust mothers because they can't keep a roof over your head or food in your belly, and to top it off, they sleep around. Not surprisingly, their relationship was strained. Whenever we returned to Richmond to visit relatives, Dad would take fifteen minutes out of our two-day trip to see Irene. I grew up thinking fifteen-minute visits with your mother on the way out of town were a great way to have a relationship with a parent in your adult years. I know—just one of the many flavors of my bruised emotional imprints.

Those imprints, as we will see, get passed along. Because of the imprint his mother's actions left on him, my dad never trusted my mother, Janie. He beat her occasionally when he thought she was too flirty with another guy. He was too deep in the grips of his bruised emotional imprints to see that it was laughable to think that she would cheat on him.

My mother's childhood taught her that she wasn't lovable or powerful, so she acquiesced to those beatings for many years. It wasn't until I graduated from law school at the age of twenty-five that my mother finally stood up for herself—by hiding behind me. She told my father, "Touch me again, and I will tell Tomi. And she will make sure you never hit me again." Isn't that the exact spot a child seeks, wedged between her parents?

My mother's childhood was traumatic, too. She was the second-youngest child in a family of eight girls and one boy. After her mother died in 1945, Janie Elizabeth was abandoned on the courthouse steps in Richmond, Virginia. Her father, a truck driver, was overwhelmed by attempting to care for the children living in the home. In the end, he turned six of his children over to the state of Virginia.

My mother spent her formative years growing up in a children's home where love and kindness were hard to come by. The harsh punishment the adults doled out in the children's home was the same whether you took an extra cookie at snack time or took $1.00 out of the purse of Mrs. Adams, the lady in charge of the children's home. No matter the infraction, the child would receive a beating and spend all of Saturday sitting in a chair facing the wall.

In those years, my mother was often hungry. Every day, she took the same school lunch, a peanut butter biscuit. The other children relentlessly teased her about that lunch. Rather than face the humiliation, she often flushed the biscuit down the commode in the girls' bathroom. She would rather be hungry than humiliated.

When my mother's older sister Anne married, she was gracious enough to allow her younger sisters, my mother included, to come live with her and her new husband, Bobby. While my mother was excited about not being in the children's home anymore, this move ushered in a new era of terror.

Bobby would get drunk many nights and go looking for his younger sisters-in-law. My mother occasionally told us stories of hiding from Bobby, hoping and praying he wouldn't find her. I never learned the details of what happened; she would only say that Bobby beat her and her sisters. I suspect Bobby took other liberties with my mother and her sisters, unspeakable horrors that my mother never voiced.

Because my mother's childhood was pockmarked with unkind and loveless acts, as an older adult she gave what she didn't receive: kindness and love. First, though, she had to work out some of the hatred, which wasn't pretty.

I imagine my mother was overwhelmed with responsibility in the early years of their marriage when my dad was busy getting an advanced education. Despite having four children under age seven and no childcare, my mother supported my father by running a small grocery store and gas station. She built playpens out of soda pop crates to contain my siblings. As the youngest, I was placed in a makeshift child seat at the checkout counter or on the floor at my mother's feet. I cannot imagine the responsibility.

True to what my mother learned as a child, regardless of the mischief my two older brothers got into at the store, her punishment for them was always the same: beating them with a switch or a stick. She was only doing what she knew, however misguided or destructive. My brothers, Jerry and Mike, stout boys even as children, seemed to withstand the beatings. It was quite scary at times, and there have been lifelong repercussions for them. By the time my sister and I were old enough to cause mischief, which we did a time or two or three, my dad had graduated with his PhD and was home more. With his constant presence, the beatings stopped.

These childhood experiences left their marks on both my mom and dad, and ultimately on my siblings and me. Compounding the lessons that my parents brought to their marriage about love and power was the strain of having a child born with a rare medical condition that almost claimed her life several times. That child was me.

My temperature-control mechanism didn't work correctly for the first few years of my life. When I ate certain foods or was exposed to specific materials, such as the stuffing in my sister's stuffed animals, my temperature rose dangerously high. When a fever spiked, instead of rushing me to the emergency room, my parents packed me in ice in the bathtub. The doctors caring for me felt like that was the best treatment. As an infant, I spent a lot of time packed in ice as my parents tried to coax my little body to hold on long enough to outgrow the medical condition. Who knew that even though I don't need ice baths now, they would be in vogue in my adult years? To this day, my baths have to be hot.

My early childhood was filled with statements like these:

- We can't do that. It might make Tomi sick.
- We have to go right now. Tomi is sick.

- I am sorry we have to give away your stuffed animal collection. It makes your sister sick, so we can't keep it.

One of the messages claimed from these moments and statements was that my illness enabled me to totally control my family. There is nothing emotionally balanced about that message. These experiences twisted my understanding of love and power.

I misinterpreted many messages from my childhood. I took my parents' angst and exasperation about my medical condition and the lack of a tried-and-true treatment for restoring my good health as evidence that I was not worth saving. Not feeling worthy made me feel unlovable. They never *said* I was unlovable or I wasn't worthy. I drew that conclusion myself.

The high fevers left their mark on me, too. I suffered subtle brain damage and developed learning disabilities that only seemed to prove my existing emotional imprint of *I am not lovable as I am*. My learning difficulties made me feel "less than" across the first fifty years of my life, preventing the full blossoming of my emotional capabilities as an individual and as a leader.

I was nothing if not resilient, though. The doctors treating me as an infant told my parents I wouldn't survive past three. When I turned three, the doctors said I wouldn't make it to seven. If I did make it, I would be severely brain damaged. When my father heard that prognosis, he began looking for special educational facilities for me, discovering one in the mountains of North Carolina. That is the third reason we moved to Durham when I was four—my dad wanted me to be able to receive the special educational services I might require one day. Fortunately, I never did. I became a lifelong learner to prove the doctors wrong and counter the message that I am slow and dumb.

The learning disabilities that resulted from the brain damage led me to quit school in the second grade. I knew I wasn't like the other children in my class, and I didn't know why. Thus, I simply refused to go to school. One time when my mother drove me to school, and dropped me off at the front door, I ran right past the school and headed for home. A bold move for a second grader, don't you agree? I was hiding in my bedroom closet before my mother even pulled into the garage at our house. After that, the principal was always waiting for me outside the building. He became my escort to ensure I made it to class.

I was ashamed that I couldn't understand how to write like my classmates. I had no idea what to do about it, and no one seemed to know how to help me. Since I wasn't getting the help I needed, I staged a rebellion by quitting school in response to my situation. I ultimately returned to the second grade and finished the school year. However, my developmental disabilities haunted me for years. I have completed many degrees and certifications for the underlying purpose of proving to the world that I am not stupid.

I was not only ashamed, I was angry. I was angry at my parents for bringing me into this world. I was angry at the forces of the universe because I arrived on the planet in ill health. I was angry because I hurt my knee in high school and couldn't play collegiate volleyball. I was even angry that anger permeated every aspect of my life. That's how stuck I was in a place of emotional imbalance. When I think about what I left in my emotional wake, I cringe. For someone dedicated to building people up, I sure could use my anger to tear them down.

Looking back, I am amazed that no one ever taught me about emotional balance and its impact on personal and professional success, especially considering my father was a psychologist. The only instruction I recall receiving on managing my feelings was in one of the courses in my PhD program. In that class, we read a book on emotional quotient (EQ), similar to intelligence quotient (IQ) but for emotional intelligence. When I took the test to measure my EQ, I scored exceptionally low. That hurt, but not enough to make me change. Instead, I used one of my favorite defense mechanisms to rationalize the low score. I said, "Oh, that is just the way I am," or "I have so many other virtues, I don't need that as one." Both statements were deflectors. They allowed me to avoid addressing the real issue of my emotional imbalance caused by my bruised emotional imprints.

While I have a trunk (or two or three) full of stories of how my emotional imbalance and the emotional imbalance of my parents and siblings materialized in the world, what matters here is that you now have a snapshot of the particular brand of chaos that made up my parents' background and mine. You can also understand and appreciate the early age at which I began fermenting in a deep emotional crock. Please, don't pity me or feel sorry for me. As the rest of the story unfolds, you will see that I wouldn't be here, at this moment with you, but for these bruises. I embrace and honor each one because they brought me here, and here is a magnificent place.

Here, after all, is the place where I establish the foundation of my new method for developing emotional balance and where I offer the building blocks for each facet of the method. It's a place of profound personal and professional excellence that I couldn't have reached before now, because achieving emotional balance is the journey of emotional maturity. "Maturity is coming to terms with that other part of yourself."[2] For years, I didn't know that *other part* of myself existed. I didn't know what to do with it when I discovered it. It took me years to figure it out. With this book, I share that journey with you and show you how you can come to terms with your other part if you choose to do so. Please note, if you're a big-picture person who doesn't want to spend time on the details, or if you are not interested in the backdrop, then proceed to Section III to learn a new method for maximizing your potential by developing emotional balance. Otherwise, I invite you to join me on my journey and thus inform your own.

I tried many ladders in my efforts to climb out of the bottomless pit of anger I nearly suffocated in as a child. I read everything I could get my hands on. I wanted to discover how to tap into all my potential *quickly* to have time in this life to use every ounce of my potential. Then, at the end of my days when I stand before my maker, I could say, "I tapped into all my abilities; I've got nothing left, and I didn't waste any time. I'm ready."

It seems I have always been driven by a desire to tap into all my potential, though I suspect that much of the fuel for that drive came from years of trying to learn information that my damaged brain simply couldn't process. Rather than give up, I reframed this experience with a question: "How *do* I access all my potential?"

I grew up believing my life span would be short, so my next question was, "How do I access all my potential *quickly*?" Are you starting to see how the bruises can make for better conversations?

Although I didn't appreciate or understand it during most of the journey, I was asking these questions in pursuit of my best self. I discovered that my best self was waiting for me at the intersection of these disciplines: emotional intelligence, leadership, and self-help. Underlying these disciplines and powering my performance in them was emotional balance. The gift of achieving emotional balance is the ability to operate from *true nature*—the sacred space of the genuine Tomi White Bryan and not the one controlled by some bruised emotional imprints formed by bumping against unwritten rules.

That genuine Tomi White Bryan is a magical, creative ball of energy with infinite possibilities as she authentically expresses her unique personality. Life is filled with effortless joy, unlimited abundance, and good health in this space. Actualizing my true nature through emotional balance was the key to accessing all my capabilities as a human being to be the best leader possible and the best human possible.

You CAN Get There from Here

Your journey to emotional balance will be different from mine, but as I captured what I saw along my journey, I realized I was building a map that could help guide others. This map is the key to the land I call Emotional Intelligence 3.0 ($EI^{3.0}$). It is the next leap in the evolution of emotional intelligence. Figure 2 illustrates this method.

$EI^{3.0}$ is the system for the efficient and effective development of high EQ. It maps the journey to high emotional intelligence through emotional balance and it offers the vehicle you need to get there. Along the way, we'll identify all the action taking place under the hood of emotional intelligence and come to see the emotional balance "engine" driving your EQ score. That engine is identified and explained by The Model of Emotional Development, the heart of EI$^{3.0}$. I discuss this model in greater detail in later chapters.

EMOTIONAL INTELLIGENCE 3.0

The **Model of Emotional Development** captures the dynamics taking place as one matures from the adapted identity to true nature across five states that track emotional balance from the state of Protection to the state of Presenced Wholeness (the most balanced emotional state).

Organizing Principle
SYSTEM DYNAMICS

True nature as a magical, creative ball of energy with infinite possibilities is achieved by maturing to the emotional state of Presenced Wholeness, resulting in emotional balance and a full blossoming of capabilities— bruised emotional imprints have been refined so they guide instead of guard.

MODEL OF EMOTIONAL DEVELOPMENT
TRUE NATURE

Organizing Principle
CREATION DYNAMICS

9 INDICATORS

Love
Anger
Release
Power
Resistance
Individuality
Energy
Awareness
Language

Presenced Wholeness
Silence & Oneness
Integration
Expression
Protection

5 EMOTIONAL STATES

Organizing Principle
SPIRAL DYNAMICS

Emotional State Indicator

A person liberates true nature from the adapted identity by maturing toward emotional balance across **nine indicators**.

The Emotional State Indicator assesses your emotional state by measuring the maturity level through the nine indicators.

ADAPTED IDENTITY

Organizing Principle
ENERGY DYNAMICS

The **adapted identity** is the personality you were forced to make up to stay safe and belong. It consists of the two bruised emotional imprints of *I am not lovable as I am* and *I am not powerful as I am* and the *comfort zone* they establish. These bruised emotional imprints are shaped by the unwritten rule of *it's not safe to be who I am (so I must be something else, and the system will dictate what that is).*

Figure 2. Emotional Intelligence 3.0.

What EI$^{3.0}$ does, that has not been done before, is to capture the dynamics of emotional development that occur as one emotionally matures from adapted identity to true nature, which is the place of emotional balance. The adapted identity consists of the two bruised emotional imprints we'll be talking about in this book:

- *I am not lovable as I am.*
- *I am not powerful as I am.*

These bruised emotional imprints create boundaries around our lives and dictate how we love ourselves and how we exercise power. These boundaries create a space for us to live in that we'll also be talking about in this book: the *comfort zone.*

These imprints and the resulting *comfort zone* are forged out of abiding by this unwritten rule: *It's not safe to be who I am (so I must be something else, and the system will dictate what that is).*

The "bruised" identity reveals itself via the inauthentic expression of the made-up personality. True nature reveals itself via the authentic expression of the unique personality, where emotional imprints guide instead of guard. These opposites are discussed in Chapter 5.

The Road Home

Following is a preview of the places you'll explore on your journey while using this book as your guide.

Organizing Principles

- System Dynamics
- Spiral Dynamics
- Creation Dynamics
- Energy Dynamics

Each principle is explained in Chapter 4.

The Nine Indicators of Emotional Balance

- Love
- Anger
- Release
- Power
- Resistance
- Individuality
- Energy
- Awareness
- Language

Indicators are defined in Chapter 6. The organic development path from imbalance to balance for each indicator is tracked and explained in Chapters 7–11. The maturity level of these nine indicators collectively reveals an emotional state.

The Five Emotional States

- Protection
- Expression
- Integration

- Silence & Oneness
- Presenced Wholeness

Chapter 6 introduces the dynamics that occur in each state. Then there is a state-by-state explanation of the organic, emotional, development process in chapters 7–11.

You can locate yourself in the EI$^{3.0}$ system using the following Emotional State Indicator.

The Emotional State Indicator (ESI)

The ESI is an assessment that measures the maturity level of the nine indicators, which reveals the emotional state and the level of emotional balance. Once you locate yourself after the assessment, you can grow from there.

Emotional Evolution

Transformation in EI$^{3.0}$ seeks to take advantage of the dynamics happening across an emotional state, which makes it easier to evolve, so you can maximize your potential efficiently and effectively. It is comprehensive enough to describe emotional evolution as it occurs. It also conveys how to achieve emotional balance so that it is possible to replicate that evolution yourself. It is the pathway to all the goodness you came here to be.

I believe EI$^{3.0}$ is a new solution to some age-old challenges, but it's not a quick fix; it requires time and commitment. Don't worry if you don't understand all the components of EI$^{3.0}$ just yet. I explain the components in the remaining chapters, including the model at its center.

Is This Book for You?

My initial offering of EI$^{3.0}$ is to leadership coaches. This audience typically consists of lifelong learners with a growth mindset. They seek methods that enhance personal and professional excellence.

That said, almost everyone on Earth can benefit from participating in this process. If you aren't aligned with the above audience, it doesn't mean you can't read this book or use EI$^{3.0}$. By all means, please read away, and thank you for being here.

If you are a coach, it is important to realize that you can't take your clients somewhere you haven't been. If you want to take your clients to the place of emotional balance, so they can fully express their personal and leadership excellence, you have to go there first. Fortunately for you, I have been there to blaze the trail.

EI$^{3.0}$ is based on having been there. At one time, I fully abided by the unwritten rule of life that *it's not safe to be who I am (so I must be something else, and the system will dictate what that is)*. I was out of balance emotionally, lost in a sea of anger, undermining my own personal and leadership capabilities. Not so much anymore. I recognize it's a journey, so there is always room for more development.

The reward of developing emotional balance is the discovery of your true nature, which leads to a life filled with effortless joy, unlimited abundance, and good health. Did you know that these rewards are your birthright as a human? They are. However, our bruised emotional imprints block our ability to see, know, and feel this truth. I reclaimed this birthright using EI$^{3.0}$. If you seek to reclaim yours, you can use this method, too. Once you do so, you can turn toward your clients and help them do the same. And that is the better conversation those bruises were made for.

TOMI'S TAKEAWAYS from This Chapter

- Many of us live by the unwritten rule of life that *it's not safe to be who I am (so I must be something else, and the system will dictate what that is)*.

- Bumping up against the limits of this rule creates the two bruised emotional imprints of *I am not lovable as I am* and *I am not powerful as I am*.

- Bruised means imbalanced.

- Bruised emotional imprints guard us, ensuring we remain within the *comfort zone* established by the unwritten rule.

- Bruised emotional imprints also mask that we are magical, creative balls of energy with infinite possibilities.

- EI$^{3.0}$ provides a map for the road home to emotional balance.

- The gift of achieving emotional balance is the ability to operate from true nature—the sacred space of effortless joy, unlimited abundance, and good health.

Chapter Two

THE BETTER
CONVERSATION

One of the bruises I received from my experiences with the *it's not safe to be who I am (so I must be something else, and the system will dictate what that is)* rule is that it wasn't safe in my family to be stupid, so you better be really, really damn smart. As a child with learning disabilities, you can imagine how that worked out for me in the early years. When I didn't understand something or needed to know more on a topic, such as tapping into more of my potential faster and more effectively, I would search for answers in a book, a workshop, a certification, or a degree. Learning has been my go-to strategy for half a century.

In 1999 I went to work for a company as its general counsel. As I watched the dynamics among the senior leadership, I thought to myself, *This cannot be what great leadership looks like, so what does it look like?* You know where I went for my answers. I read books on leadership and participated in a leadership development program sponsored by the chamber of commerce in my hometown. *Leadership Greensboro* was a fascinating program that only made me want to understand more about leadership. Shortly after the program ended, I decided to earn a PhD in leadership. Through my studies, I discovered that leaders could be developed but that exceptional leadership is rare. I also realized that the leadership I witnessed in my company had room for improvement—and don't we all?

In 2005 I earned my PhD. I spent the next few years exploring ways to promote leadership capabilities in others. I also developed my leadership skills by obtaining certifications and designations related to leadership.

My takeaway from those educational experiences? I concluded that being a better leader was about being a better person. But how? You won't be surprised to hear I spent the next decade trying to understand how to become a better person. I read a truckload of books, attended more workshops, and earned more certifications.

As happened with the leadership skills, I seemed to plateau at a certain point in my development journey, and I struggled to tap into the outer edges of my gifts and talents. The three disciplines of leadership, self-help, and emotional intelligence include impressive materials and a multitude of learning opportunities. Still, I felt like those disciplines took me only so far and then left me hanging. For instance, in the leadership discipline, the most compelling research indicates that leaders can be categorized as bad, good, or great, and that great leaders bring significantly more profit to an organization than others.[3] Great leaders, according to the research, scored in the top 10 percent on a 360-feedback assessment, which meant they possessed at least five strengths at the ninetieth percentile.[4] The proposed path for reaching this level of greatness was self-development and massive doses of feedback.

I found these insights on leadership compelling. I also had some questions. Chiefly, how does one put that information into practice effectively and efficiently? As someone who has six strengths at the ninetieth percentile on a 360-feedback assessment, I didn't feel like I'd achieved greatness. There was still background noise on my assessment and in my life that needed my attention. I thought the research was missing something crucial, and I wanted to understand what it was.

I felt like I had exhausted what was available to me in the leadership and self-help disciplines. Unsure what to do next, I pondered living in an ashram for a year to continue my self-development, but I wasn't ready to be away from my husband, my children, and my beloved black lab, Mojo, for that long. Instead, I rediscovered emotional intelligence as a way to close the perceived gaps in my capabilities.

While exploring leadership and self-help, I read a backpack's worth of books on emotional intelligence and EQ. As part of my exploration in the fall of 2020, I revisited emotional intelligence. I even obtained a certification in the EQ-i$^{2.0}$, the most popular EQ assessment at the time. As I reengaged this discipline, my perspective shifted. I realized that emotional intelligence is the platform for leadership and self-help.

I began to see that, without makeup on, emotional intelligence is your ability to recognize and allow your feelings and the feelings of others without being triggered by them. Doing so enables us to engage in balanced exchanges with the world. When we dress it up and send it out in the world to play, emotional intelligence becomes complex and complicated, but it doesn't have to be. It is within your power to achieve emotional balance using EI$^{3.0}$.

On my second ride-along with emotional intelligence, I noticed that leadership, self-help, and emotional intelligence development approaches usually focus on behavioral outputs: Am I happy? Am I a positive person? Am I a collaborator? Am I good at social relationships? Am I trustworthy? Am I a visionary? I observed that simply coaching someone on outputs was not the most effective, long-term solution for excelling. That type of coaching doesn't consider the powerful force behind our actions and related feelings: our unprocessed emotional experiences.

Tapping into the power of my bruised emotional imprints, I explored the dynamics taking place below the surface of emotional intelligence. Doing so offered me an entirely new perspective— I realized that it was all about balance. All systems seek balance. Our emotional system is no different. Maybe reaching my potential wasn't about redlining my leadership capabilities after all. Perhaps it was about finding balance. Unfortunately, most of us don't develop an appreciation for the value of balance or what it means for our feelings. I certainly hadn't when I started my journey.

EI$^{3.0}$ offers a way to reframe EQ and emotional intelligence. It answers the call to reorganize the paradigms by which we are living. With this book, I invite you to find emotional balance for yourself so that effortless joy, unlimited abundance, and good health are your constant companions, and the companions of the people you coach on the road of life. Achieve emotional balance and live your gifts and talents to the fullest. It is a place of profound personal and professional success.

A Frame of Reference for Emotional Intelligence

My brother, Dr. Jerry White, introduces new students to psychology by familiarizing them with the three Qs. Jerry tells them that humans are composed of three quotients: a physical quotient (PQ), an intelligence quotient (IQ), and an emotional quotient (EQ). While you can never reduce anyone to just six letters, using the concepts of PQ, IQ, and EQ allows Jerry to introduce complex topics to his students easily. I will use his model here to introduce you to emotional intelligence.

Our society tends to hold IQ and PQ above EQ. Most of us are keenly aware that there is an ideal range of IQ, for instance. People do not want to be perceived as not smart enough or as too smart. Yes, elements of society will impose consequences for being overly brilliant. Many of us seek strategies to improve grades and educational performance, because the unwritten rule and its enforcers send us messages that our IQ, whatever it may be, is not ideal. And yet, it's challenging to change your IQ. While people can be taught how to think more effectively to improve grades or performance, IQ remains static across a life span.

Our PQ is much the same. Many of us seek to change our physical appearance, because the unwritten rule and its enforcers send us messages that our PQ, whatever we may look like, is not ideal. Most people do not want to be perceived as not pretty enough or as too pretty. Yes, elements of society will impose consequences for being overly beautiful.

While a person can make specific changes to their physical appearance through beauty routines, fitness workouts, dieting, and plastic surgery, their physique isn't much more malleable than their IQ. That physique is encoded into their DNA and primarily reflects that inherited structure. I am not saying that changes to physical appearance aren't possible. I am just saying that achieving such alterations can take a lot of effort. If you have been overweight like I have been, determining what food lifestyle agrees with your bodily systems can be challenging, time-consuming, and frustrating.

In the way someone else might swoon over a high IQ or a high PQ, I swoon over high EQ. An EQ score is a measurement of how you use the outputs of emotional intelligence in positive ways. Though your IQ and PQ tend to remain stable throughout your life, your EQ can improve. You can have a *profound* impact on your EQ.

There are EQ assessments and emotional intelligence frameworks and models that can help you improve performance in this quotient. Still, the current methods don't meet my requirement of offering a systemic solution. My perspective doesn't make any of those methods bad, wrong, or invalid. It just means they don't suit me and how I show up in the world.

Throughout my career, I have seen and experienced the consequences of continuing to engage feelings in traditional ways that only address the outputs of emotional intelligence. One of those consequences is that we unwittingly create a default future for ourselves rather than reach new heights. Our bruised emotional imprints want our worlds to stay the same, holding us in a *comfort zone*, and their influence can be powerful, insidious, and invisible. Even as those bruised imprints are busy running our lives, most of us have no clue they do so. We may go to bed tonight filled with hopes and dreams of a better tomorrow, but the default future determined by our bruised emotional imprints doesn't allow space for anything new. That means that today will be just like yesterday, and tomorrow will be just like today. You know the drill: "Same shit, different day."

Every single time we unknowingly default to those bruised emotional imprints, we become more tightly locked in the same place. When we do so over and over, we project the past into the future again and again. The trance is hard to break; highly trained professionals can't reliably lift the veil, so think how our clients must feel.

An Imbalanced Society

Imbalance is deeply ingrained in our culture. When we fully live in the clutches of imbalance, our bruised emotional imprints are totally in charge of the show. In this place, anger's action is a destructive force. As author and activist Parker J. Palmer says, "Violence is what happens when we don't know what else to do with our suffering."[5]

Jerry Colonna, a coach to leaders and entrepreneurs, expands on the reason for violence, writing that "violence to our planet, violence to our communities, and violence to ourselves are what we do when we refuse to look inward and work with the heartbreak of the everyday."[6] Such violence occurs because, in the clutches of emotional imbalance, we allow our anger to project "out onto others in destructive and often violent ways. It's used to belittle and hurt. We don't just feel wronged, we want revenge."[7]

The American legal system's origins are rooted in a system seeking balance. Sometimes that's difficult to see because the people of the United States and the system itself have perverted the system, making it punitive and vindictive rather than balanced. Because people have been so profoundly hurt, and remain mired in that pain, they don't demand balanced justice. Instead, they demand justice that hurts the alleged offender the same way they have been harmed. The old "an eye for an eye" method doesn't make for a balanced society. It makes for a blind one.

People who actualize the most balanced emotional state of Presenced Wholeness accept that justice means balance, not vengeance. They recognize that the true purpose of a murder trial is to create balance in the system, not to punish people. A life for a life is not balanced; it is vengeance rooted in overwhelming anger. A life for the four lives that a criminal may have taken is still not balanced. When the justice system takes a person's life, the right to seek repair of the harm inflicted is forever taken away, and the system remains imbalanced. As an advocate of system balance, I can no longer support the death penalty.

However, allowing a person the opportunity to transform in their way—to repent, find forgiveness, and seek balance for the imbalanced acts committed? That I support wholeheartedly.

We perpetuate imbalance outside the justice system, too. The problem is getting worse as cyberspace, mainly through social media platforms, encourages and fosters emotional imbalance. It gives those with less-than-good intentions a new playing field for triggering, inciting, invoking, and inviting people who are not in a place of emotional balance to form personal alliances that are unlikely in service of the greater good. The emotional free fall in cyberspace gets carried over into people's daily interactions in the real world. Think of the insurrection on January 6, 2021, in Washington, DC—most of that event was organized online but carried out in person.

While I see the number of people in the most imbalanced emotional states growing, I don't see the world developing effective countermeasures. If we are not mindful, online shaming, cyberbullying, road rage, and unprecedented gun violence will continue to grow. Without a healthier option, society cannot continue to evolve. *For the world to reach its potential, we must transform our feelings to move toward emotional balance, not away from it.*

The core of this growing challenge is that most of us never learned effective methods for engaging our feelings. We have little or no space left for learning them now because our emotional wells are filled with unprocessed feelings from yesterday, last week, and long ago. Plus, the world keeps piling on new experiences that have nowhere to go. Without the proper tools, we indiscriminately spew outward. Worse, others who are not interested in advancing the greater good can manipulate and control that spewing. Again, think of the insurrection. I offer additional examples of this behavior in Chapter 7.

Turning the Emotional Tides

Established methods of increasing emotional intelligence are not leading us in the direction we need to go at an appropriate pace. We need approaches that will move people to a more balanced emotional state. It doesn't have to hurt; we can do it with precision, simplicity, ease, and grace. But we must do it. If society is to continue to evolve emotionally, we need to transform the way we engage our feelings.

To make such a profound change, we must turn the emotional tides in the same way we seek to turn the tides of environmental harm to the planet. As we figure out new ways to love ourselves and express our power, we can see new ways to do the same for each other and for the planet. It is not an either-or proposition. It is a both-and.

EI$^{3.0}$ helps us see the possibilities. It disassembles and plumbs the depths of emotional intelligence and EQ. It allows us to leverage other influences for meaningful and effective growth and transformation. Thus, instead of improving emotional intelligence outcomes, my method engages the dynamics that create those outcomes.

The power of EI$^{3.0}$ is that it addresses the underlying, root cause of low emotional intelligence: emotional imbalance created by the invisible yet controlling, out-of-balance, bruised emotional imprints that dictate who and what we are and how we show up in the world. We can finally see those deep currents that lead us astray and hold us back. EI$^{3.0}$ redefines, reconfigures, and improves the way we engage the bruised emotional imprints at the root of our emotional imbalance, paving the way for us to be who we came here to be. Not only do we stop pretending we aren't a magical, creative ball of energy with infinite possibilities, we fully embrace being that.

Too Good to Be True?

The vision of the future I am sharing may seem too good to be true. We cannot easily comprehend such a shift when we are emotionally imbalanced. I understand the skepticism. If you had asked me when I started my journey if I believed that I was entitled to a life filled with effortless joy, unlimited abundance, and good health, I would have emphatically replied no with some other spicy words thrown in for style points. I was deeply committed to pretending I was not a magical, creative ball of energy.

Yet, speaking from experience, I can assure you that effortless joy, unlimited abundance, and good health are part of the inheritance of emotional balance. EI$^{3.0}$ reveals the path to that magical place where the emotionally balanced life of your dreams awaits you. Walking that path allows you to learn a new and proven method for increasing your emotional intelligence. Walking the path also counters the increasing number of people whose emotional imbalance contributes to rising violence, cyberbullying, cancel culture, and other negative social trends.

Why do I think redesigning how we develop and mature emotional intelligence is the antidote to some of the current disempowering and hurtful cultural trends and our limiting emotional imprints? That might be the most straightforward question to answer in this book. It's because the impact of high emotional intelligence and a resulting high EQ is sweeping and comprehensive. High EQ is rewarding and positively impacts many aspects of an individual's personal and professional life. Entrepreneur and strategist Abhi Golhar writes that emotional intelligence is not just a trend:

Major companies have compiled statistical proof that employees with emotional intelligence affect the bottom line. In fact, companies with employees that have high levels of emotional intelligence see major increases in total sales and productivity.

In a competitive workplace, developing your EQ skills is vital to your professional success.[8]

The skills associated with high EQ significantly impact the person who has the high EQ, those who are in a relationship with that person, and the organization that employs that person.

Every human can reap the rewards of a high EQ by developing emotional balance. Dr. Travis Bradberry, a pioneer in the emotional intelligence discipline, offered these insights on its impact:

- Your emotional intelligence is the foundation for a host of critical skills—it impacts most everything you say and do each day.
- Emotional intelligence is the single biggest predictor of performance in the workplace and the strongest driver of leadership and personal excellence.
- 90% of top performers are also high in emotional intelligence. On the flip side, just 20% of bottom performers are high in emotional intelligence. You can be a top performer without emotional intelligence, but the chances are slim.
- People with a high degree of emotional intelligence make more money—an average of $29,000 more per year than people with a low degree of emotional intelligence.
- The link between emotional intelligence and earnings is so direct that every point increase in emotional intelligence adds $1,300 to an annual salary.
- These findings hold true for people in all industries, at all levels, in every region of the world. We haven't yet been able to find a job in which performance and pay aren't tied closely to emotional intelligence.[9]

The reverberations of high emotional intelligence in a person's life are astounding.

The highest level of emotional intelligence in EI$^{3.0}$ occurs in the emotional state of Integration. After Integration, the importance of emotional intelligence fades as a person evolves toward divine balance and emotional balance. Presenced Wholeness is the most balanced emotional state. It is also a rarity. Based on research on adult development, it is estimated that about half of 1 percent of the world's population is emotionally balanced. I don't offer that statistic to dampen anyone's enthusiasm. Instead, I use it to show that there is plenty of opportunity to realize immediate and impactful shifts in emotional balance. Isn't that a beautiful thought?

Make New Choices, Get New Results

As you contemplate making your emotional balance journey, it is important to appreciate that every choice you make creates results: intended and unintended.

By far, one of the significant, ongoing results for me is unexpected and unprecedented levels of joy. I have never been happier, and that is a direct result of knowing that other people's reactions to me reflect their level of emotional balance. I am not responsible for anyone's emotional well-being but my own. Don't get me wrong. I am not a Grinch or a Scrooge who steals joy from others. I have bad days, but I love seeing other people happy. Now, the difference is that I seek to source my actions from balance. I also appreciate that I can't change anyone else—only myself. I can invite others to join my journey, but I can't make them evolve.

Another unexpected outcome of choosing to develop emotional balance is the freedom that comes with it. When I realized that I didn't have to spend my energy trying to make other people happy, I freed up energy to continue growing my joy, abundance, and health. I have seen improvements in my overall health because I am no longer an emotional eater. While I can't offer you a 100 percent money-back guarantee that these results will occur for you as a consequence of reaching emotional balance, I feel confident that if you choose this path, you are saying yes to embracing positive, new ways of being in the world. It's a great space, and I welcome you.

That said, you should also know that not everyone will be happy for you. People don't always like it when you change. As you begin to align with your true nature, others face a dilemma: Do they develop, too, or do they hold you in this spot, so they don't have to do anything because they are unaware or afraid? Most people choose the latter.

First, people may become ugly toward you and try to nail your foot to the floor. You will likely hear others say something such as, "I don't even know who you are anymore." Such comments are intended, consciously or unconsciously, to stop you from developing.

Second, some people can hold the space for you to mature emotionally without changing themselves. The person who can do this is likely already on the path of developing emotional balance or has a commitment to the development of others as a coach, counselor, leader, mentor, teacher, or someone in a similar profession.

Third, sometimes you have to choose to let people off your bus. Some people just can't make the journey with you. This is not a good thing or a bad thing. It just is. You must have the courage to let them off your bus at the next stop—and letting go can be difficult.

Dr. David Hawkins, an authority within the fields of consciousness research and spirituality, offered these insights on the impact your transformation can have on relationships:

> Paradoxically, such breakthroughs and expansions may be upsetting to friends and family members because of the shift of balance. Things that we had done out of constriction, fear, guilt, or a sense of duty may be suddenly thrown overboard… Safety and security become less important than discovery and exploration. Personal lives pick up momentum, and movement replaces stuck-in-a-rut life patterns.[10]

Truthfully, seeking emotional balance is a personal journey that many people opt not to take. Usually, they are unaware of the possible journey, or if they are aware of the journey, they have no idea how to begin. Most of us tend to walk the familiar path because it seems more manageable; it's the path of least resistance. I make no judgment if you opt not to take the journey, although the fact that you are reading this book indicates that you are already on your way. The idea that it's possible to live an emotionally balanced life filled with effortless joy, unlimited abundance, and good health can be surprisingly scary, activating all sorts of roadblocks and barriers that seek to keep us locked in place.

On the other hand, the upside can be tremendous. The emotional balance journey will bring many spectacular gifts into your world that you didn't anticipate or even recognize as possible. One of those gifts is a higher level of consciousness. There is a direct correlation between a more mature, emotional state and higher states of consciousness, also called enlightenment, utopia, Shangri-la, Xanadu, or being "woke." We'll explore more about these mind-expanding possibilities in later chapters.

What Emotional Balance Is Not

For now, though, let's be clear about what developing your emotional balance is not. It is not about becoming a snowflake, a cream puff, a cupcake, or a crybaby—and my apologies for the labeling.

Emotional balance is not easy to accomplish. This work will be some of the hardest of your life. You'll meet plenty of resistance. Stepping into all that you came here to be is a radical act of self-love and self-power that the forces behind the unwritten rule will try to prevent. Your ego will invoke its most brilliant defense mechanisms to keep you locked in the familiar. Thus, this journey is not about becoming soft. It's about becoming a force for good in the way that only you can. Doing so takes bravery and courage, especially if you are like most of us and didn't have emotionally balanced parents who knew how to model simple and effective methods for processing life's many overwhelming events. There is no judgment here. They couldn't model Presenced Wholeness if they never learned it themselves, and our world is simply not proficient at teaching us what to do with our feelings and how to hold them in balanced ways. If your parents modeled Presenced Wholeness for you, I am jealous and grateful that you had that experience. And if it wasn't modeled for you, then welcome to the club. I am delighted you are here. We are on this journey together.

A Word on Momentum

Be aware that it can be tough to stop once you start going down this rabbit hole, like Alice in Wonderland. Exploring further is not a bad thing, either. It just means that once you open yourself up to the adventure, don't be surprised if you end up going all the way to Presenced Wholeness.

My journey of emotional balance took me on a ride that lasted more than twenty years. In the beginning, I had no idea what I was pursuing. I had no exact set of instructions or a map of where I was going. I just sensed I was on a new path. I knew the life I was leading wasn't fulfilling, despite my happiness with my husband and my two sons, so I set off without a North Star in view, veering right or left when it felt appropriate.

The search became all-consuming. I read over two thousand books. I sought help from anyone I thought might have answers. I attended workshops and got certifications in all sorts of disciplines. I made appointments with traditional counselors and therapists, spiritual counselors, psychics, Reiki masters, soul coaches, and past-life regression coaches. I even fire-walked by the light of the moon on a beach in California. I felt commanded by some unseen force to explore and excavate the depths of my soul. My family might have described me as obsessed. I only knew that I needed answers about life. I struggled to find them in a language I could comprehend and apply to my life. Still, I had to keep going. I did warn you that going down this rabbit hole would compel you to continue the journey.

Each time I felt like I had "arrived" somewhere new on the journey, I wrote a book about it. I called it self-help because the experience had no other logical name. Those books are a very public account of my journey to emotional balance. I was brazen enough—the word arrogant might be a better fit—after writing each book to think I was finished with the journey, but the universe had other plans for me.

Each of my books was a stepping-stone on the path of emotional balance. I wrote this book from the other side of those experiences. To paraphrase Danish philosopher and existentialist Søren Kierkegaard, "Life can only be understood backwards; but it must be lived forwards."

I no longer proclaim I am at the end of the journey. Although, with this book, I admit nearing the end feels truer than it ever has before. But what do I know? All I can do is keep showing up to see what happens, and maybe one day, all will be revealed. Now, more than ever, I do appreciate the benefit of hindsight. I can reflect upon my experiences, understand them better, and organize them into something meaningful for others who also desire to be emotionally balanced.

Whatever you seek, even if you don't have a name for it, here is a good place where you can start your journey with $EI^{3.0}$.

As American philosopher and mythologist Joseph Campbell said, "The privilege of a lifetime is being who you are."[11] That has undoubtedly been accurate for me. I humbly offer you $EI^{3.0}$ as a transformational system you can use to become who you are and model the beauty of that for the world to appreciate and emulate.

May the magic you create as you develop emotional balance using $EI^{3.0}$ take you places and bring you people and experiences that exceed your wildest dreams. There is work to be done, tears to be shed, and joy to be experienced.

TOMI'S TAKEAWAYS from This Chapter

- For the world to reach its potential, we must transform our feelings to move toward emotional balance, not away from it.

- High EQ is rewarding and positively impacts many aspects of an individual's personal and professional life.

- Our bruised emotional imprints create and sustain a "Same shit, different day" experience.

- With EI$^{3.0}$, we can finally see the deep currents that lead us astray and hold us back.

- Choosing to step into all you came here to be is a radical act of self-love and self-power that the forces behind the unwritten rule will try to prevent.

- Once you start down the path of emotional balance, you may not want to stop until you reach Presenced Wholeness.

THE BACKDROP OF EMOTIONAL BALANCE

Chapter Three

SHIFTING THE FOCUS

The field of emotional intelligence is still evolving. We continue to learn how to play the game and understand the rules. Because of the positive impact emotional intelligence has on all aspects of daily life, finding more meaningful methods for increasing emotional intelligence seems imperative.

In this chapter, I describe some of the ways EI$^{3.0}$ differs from current models of emotional intelligence and explain how this shift unfolded. It is essential to acknowledge that we can travel in new directions because of what has been discovered and described in the field of emotional intelligence thus far. Today, we find ourselves able to take shortcuts, such as EI$^{3.0}$, only because of the hard work of so many others who saw the importance of emotional intelligence and began investigating what it was and how it works.

Current models of emotional intelligence identify the outputs of emotional intelligence and seek to improve performance on those outputs. Outputs include capacities like stress tolerance, independence, assertiveness, and optimism. This output-focused approach, while helpful, doesn't address the root cause of low emotional intelligence. Such an approach will ultimately falter because the underlying reasons for low performance haven't been resolved. $EI^{3.0}$ shifts the focus of development to the leverage points of emotional balance and away from the outputs of emotional intelligence.

$EI^{3.0}$ is novel. It isn't about strategies and tactics for improving performance on an output. Traditional strategies and tactics of emotional intelligence are about treating the symptoms. Leaving the root cause of those symptoms unaddressed results in a high risk of recurrence of them. You learned how to be more optimistic or assertive and, at this moment, your feelings are now front and center, ready to run or ruin your life, and what do you do about that? $EI^{3.0}$ aims to resolve the root cause of low emotional intelligence, so that symptoms disappear for good—and you become that which you already are, the you that the world so desperately needs.

I am not saying that you can't raise your emotional intelligence with current methods or that it is wrong to do so. You can absolutely increase your emotional intelligence with conventional methods. I view that as taking the scenic route, though, and I am not a scenic route kind of gal. I want to go from point A to point B in the most efficient and most effective route possible, using all the available shortcuts. From my perspective, $EI^{3.0}$ is that route.

My penchant for shortcuts was partially rooted in the childhood experiences of working for my father. My psychologist dad had a home office in the late 1970s and 1980s, before home offices were a thing. Along with my three siblings, I had to work as his receptionist a few times a week. I remember watching people come to his office for months or years at a time. From my inexperienced vantage point, it appeared that sometimes his clients made progress, but sometimes, they didn't.

As I got older and needed help myself, I became frustrated by traditional approaches to personal development. I didn't want to spend three years on a couch, as my dad's clients did. I knew there had to be better ways for people to move past long-standing hurts, traumas, and wounds, to find the authentic self within—says the woman who took more than twenty years to crack the nut.

$EI^{3.0}$ is rooted in my real-life, grounded attempts to understand how the world of human endeavors operates. It is not an abstract archetype based on wishes, hopes, and dreams. It is based on a life-time of experiences, many of them not so pretty. I burned bridges; let go of people and circled back on those people; made inflammatory statements (remind me to introduce you to my flamethrower persona sometime); quit school in the second grade; attempted to leave my husband (several times); had skin cancer and lost loved ones to other types of cancer; walked away from jobs and changed careers entirely; lost $370,000 in a cyber fraud scheme; almost lost my son to appendicitis; had appendicitis myself in my fifties; almost died several times (not due to the appendicitis); almost lost my brother to substance abuse; experienced a miscarriage; practiced being a fire-breathing dragon (and have you met my warrior bitch persona?); shouldered the financial responsibility of caring for my invalid mother and sick brother; earned a law degree and a PhD, only to be told years later that I am overqualified in job interviews; and on and on. When I say "almost lost" my son and my brother, I mean those two leaned over into death's abyss and took a long look before deciding it was better to remain above ground on Earth.

Thus, $EI^{3.0}$ is based on what I repeatedly have seen work in the face of a lifetime of ups and downs. This book describes my phenomenological study of human endeavors and the development of emotional balance. I haven't lived a charmed life (although the view from my backyard porch is pretty magical). I have lived a damned good adventure, and it has taught me a great deal about the way emotional balance develops and operates. I invite you to join me on parts of my journey, to show you how I built each facet of $EI^{3.0}$ and connected them to bring to life The Model of Emotional Development.

It is important to me to share how $EI^{3.0}$ and its processes align and influence each other because in personal development:

> Unexpected great leaps may very well occur at any time, and all students should be advantaged by having the necessary information of what to know at certain points along the way. The knowledge that is needed at 'the end' is essential right from the 'beginning.'[12]

I want you to have the entire backdrop of $EI^{3.0}$, so you have the information you need from the beginning. If a process doesn't make sense now, don't worry; it eventually will.

For now, I am not asking you to believe in $EI^{3.0}$ and the greater processes at work within it. I am asking you to suspend disbelief. As author Dr. Rachel Naomi Remen writes, "Sometimes knowing life requires us to suspend disbelief, to recognize that all our hard-won knowledge may only be provisional and the world may be quite different than we believe it to be."[13] Besides, it's good practice: developing emotional balance requires continually adjusting your lenses. I understand how disorienting it can feel to start on this journey. Almost nothing made sense when I began my inquiries, but that only drove me to ask more questions. When I read something that seemed important, but I didn't understand how it might show up in the world, I asked, "What does that look like?" Every concept shared in this book resulted from my attempts to answer that question.

Years into the search for my best self, I still had more questions than answers. Not finding answers became incredibly frustrating for me, driving me to find better solutions for myself and for those seeking to make a journey of self-discovery. I was relentless about it, too, and possibly even a snarky jackbutt every time I discovered a new idea that didn't include a tool with it that showed me exactly how to execute the idea. I sought processes that worked in a reasonable amount of time. I sought approaches that came with a map, a worksheet, a diagram, or a checklist. I sought methods that let me see where I was on the journey and where I still had to go. I wanted processes that took me on a trip to a fantastic place. Because I couldn't find those methods or see them already in the world, I built them, connecting dots in ways others didn't. The result is $EI^{3.0}$. I hope that it prevents my unsatisfying experiences from happening to you.

A New Foundation: Systems Thinking

The effectiveness of $EI^{3.0}$ originates from the transparency that this unified field theory provides. It clearly articulates the root cause of low emotional intelligence and the leverage points that influence that root cause, engaging these aspects with more satisfying and sustained results. When root causes and leverage points are the focal points for transformation, shifts occur more efficiently and effectively. Learning why you get angry is more helpful than being told to calm down, isn't it?

This transparency is possible because of systems thinking. So that we stand on common ground, I offer a brief overview of what systems thinking is and how it works.

Systems thinking is a way to operationalize seeing the lifecycle of interconnected elements to build the system; it is a liberating structure. I learned about systems thinking in 2003 when I was working on my PhD. I wanted to write a dissertation on how people ignore the warning signals that typically precede a crisis. The crisis I wanted to write about involved a factory explosion that killed several employees.

As I explained my idea to my dissertation committee on a telephone call, one member commented that he didn't think I would be able to get permission to conduct the appropriate research. Various governmental agencies, lawyers, and experts were involved in the case, so I would need their permission to conduct my research. He suggested an alternative topic: a case study applying systems thinking to crisis management. I wasn't thrilled with his idea, probably because it wasn't mine. However, I didn't want to delay completing my dissertation. I got permission to pursue the second topic if my first choice didn't work out.

Of course, my initial idea didn't work out. When I started hearing only silence from potential research subjects, due to lawsuits being in full swing, I knew I would have to change topics. That professor was so much smarter than I was. He also wisely recommended I start my research by reading Peter Senge's pivotal book *The Fifth Discipline: The*

Art & Practice of The Learning Organization. I read it and have been hooked on systems thinking ever since.

One of the most important items to know about systems thinking is that it is a multifaceted concept: "At its broadest level, systems thinking encompasses a large and fairly amorphous body of methods, tools, and principles, all oriented to looking at the interrelatedness of forces, and seeing them as part of a common process."[14] It is also considered "a discipline for seeing the 'structures' that underlie complex situations, and for discerning high from low leverage change."[15] From my perspective, systems thinking is one of the most capable tools for making transparent the complete patterns of a system to help us understand how to change the system more effectively. Application of systems thinking focuses on discovering points of high-leverage change within the system's patterns.

I applied Senge's approach in developing EI[3.0] by looking underneath the complexity of emotional intelligence, leadership, and self-help for interrelated forces to see how they came together as a shared process. I started with my own experiences. I found that it wasn't always easy to see the big picture while I was in the thick of things. Most of the time, I could only identify and give language to the experience after the fact. I'm sure that sounds familiar to you; most of us live piecemeal, managing personal crisis after personal crisis, small and large, with little end in sight. We fail to view the day-to-day happenings of our lives in the larger scheme of our personal universes.

This piecemeal approach limits development toward emotional balance in two ways. First, we do not clearly understand changing our lives more effectively. Second, most of us do not act in balance with the whole of our personal universes. Systems thinking offers a method of moving past this fragmented approach. Instead, we must seek to shift systems in a way that is aligned with the greater processes of the universe.

The first unlocking move in systems thinking is shifting away from linear cause-and-effect thinking to circular, relationship thinking. In systems, events don't necessarily happen in a straight line, one after the other. Systems thinking is conducted in a dynamic circle that reflects the interconnectedness of all the parts of the system. The preferred method for drawing a system is to use a feedback loop to reveal patterns of behavior created by the structure. This process allows us to see the interrelationships and the mutual currents of influence among the parts. "A system is a perceived whole whose elements 'hang together' because they continually affect each other over time and operate toward a common purpose."[16] A feedback loop allows these related elements of the system to emerge. EI$^{3.0}$ is a perceived whole extracted from emotional intelligence, leadership, and self-help. Its elements hang together because they continually affect each other over time as they move you toward the common purpose of developing emotional balance.

There are two essential components of the feedback loop: it has leverage points and limits, or what Senge called structural conflicts.

Leverage

A behavior that is a leverage point acts as a gas pedal. Engaging in that behavior accelerates you through the system. According to Dr. Hawkins, "In a system of considerable complexity, there is a very precise point where even a small amount of energy applied brings about a major change."[17] That is exactly what leverage points are: the places where a small amount of energy brings about a significant change.

A structural conflict is a behavior that is a counterforce in the system. Engaging in that behavior acts as a brake that prevents acceleration through the system.

Leverage points and structural conflicts tend to be opposite sides of the same coin. In building the system of $EI^{3.0}$, I sought to focus only on those elements that resulted in high-leverage change.

As I zigzagged across the fields of leadership, business, new age spirituality, self-help, emotional intelligence, and whatever else got my attention, I was constantly looking for leverage points that would accelerate my transformation. I also kept trying to understand the system in which I stood. Was it enlightenment? Self-mastery? Personal transformation? Was I even standing in any system, or was I lost in an in-between place? As Kierkegaard inferred, I had to live it and be on the other side of the experience to understand it. When I got to the other side of the journey, I understood it led me toward emotional balance.

The Performance Formula

Because of Senge's work, I began to look at the greater processes of the universe and how they influenced development toward my best self. One of the most profound discoveries I made, and the second influence on the way I think about human endeavors, is the performance formula. This formula reveals how to continually access more and more human potential through high-leverage change.

I thought this formula came from the book *The Inner Game of Tennis: The Classic Guide to the Mental Side of Peak Performance*, authored by Timothy Gallwey. For years, I attributed the performance formula to him. However, the last two times I returned to his book, I couldn't find such a formula. Whether the formula was developed by Gallwey or inspired by his book, it transformed the way I approach personal development.

The performance formula is rooted in systems thinking. It represents elements that hang together and affect each other over time while operating toward a common purpose. It also identifies points of high-leverage change. Here is the formula:

Performance = Potential minus Interference

Performance is a person's current operating level in the system, i.e., how well you are operating at this moment. Potential is the possibilities for that person: the gap between current abilities and unrealized capabilities. Interference is anything that limits or masks the ability to access one's full potential and includes those bruised emotional imprints. The more we reduce the interference, the more potential we can access, naturally increasing our performance. Improving our performance allows us to step into the next larger system waiting for us.

I relied almost exclusively on this formula for several years. It allowed me to identify the structural conflicts that minimize movement through a system and to discover the leverage points that support seeing the complexities of the system. In plain English, it helped me understand how the world of self-development worked.

The more I matured toward emotional balance, the more I realized the performance formula was only part of the story. I came to understand that knowing structural conflicts and leverage points aren't always enough to fuel transformation and growth. When I reached a more mature, emotional state, I knew I needed a better explanation.

As I matured through Expression into Integration (much more on this process in later chapters), my perspective shifted. I realized that maximizing my potential wasn't solely about reducing interference. It was also about freeing my potential. And what did that look like? It looked like the liberating structures I had learned about from Henri Lipmanowicz and Keith McCandless's book *The Surprising Power of Liberating Structures*. Lipmanowicz and McCandless write about liberating structures that

> make it easy to transform how people interact and work together in order to achieve much better results than what is possible with presentations, reports, and other conventional methods. We call them Liberating Structures because they are designed to include and engage everybody. They 'liberate,' so to speak, everybody's contribution to the group's success.[18]

I felt I had found the holy grail—the understanding that liberating structures can free the energy of the leverage point. Surely *this* was the key to unlocking a dramatic improvement in the development of emotional balance. It seemed as though I had unearthed the whole formula.

Not so fast, Tomi. As has been the case many times over on my journey to maximize my potential, just when I thought I had exhausted a particular topic or path, the universe had different plans for me. Had I solved the puzzle? Nope. Nada. *Non. Nein.* Had I found another piece of the puzzle? Yes, I found a piece that would transform the way I designed EI$^{3.0}$. But I had to be curious about one more thing: the right time to use the liberating structure to maximize its effectiveness.

As I explored timing, I realized that the path of emotional balance was paved with what I termed *emotional openings*. The emotional opening forms when space is created in a moment that, if taken advantage of, allows you to see, know, or feel the world in a new way. It shifts your paradigm so you can step into a larger system. In EI[3.0], such a shift can move you closer to emotional balance, though it is not guaranteed. For transformation to occur, a person experiencing an emotional opening must *choose* to do something different to leverage the opening.

EI[3.0] teaches us to bring together disparate and seemingly unrelated signals from our lives' broad and fuzzy patterns. It teaches us to pay attention to those signals that warn us our feelings are out of balance, taking us in a direction we probably don't want to go. When we pick up those signals, we can respond appropriately, smoothing out our evolution toward emotional balance and preventing us from blowing up our lives in the name of transformation. Amen! to that, sisters and brothers.

Because of these discoveries, I renamed and rewrote the performance formula. I now call it the Maximize Your Potential, Optimize Your Performance Formula, and it focuses on freeing energy instead of eliminating interference. This formula is the foundation for freeing all your potential or as much of it as you seek to free. See Figure 3 for the revised formula.

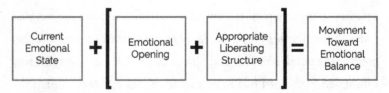

Figure 3. The Maximize Your Potential, Optimize Your Performance Formula

The takeaway from the revised formula is this: liberating structures make it easy to transform how we interact and work with our adapted identity to achieve emotional balance more effectively than conventional ideas about emotional intelligence and EQ.

It's not always easy to see how the different elements in our equation work together. As Senge writes, patterns happening in the world

> often take years to fully play out their effects on each other. Since we are part of that lacework ourselves, it's doubly hard to see the whole pattern of change. Instead, we tend to focus on snapshots of isolated parts of the system, and wonder why our deepest problems never seem to get solved.[19]

After reading this passage, I didn't feel bad about taking over twenty years to see how EI$^{3.0}$ worked. There were concepts that I simply couldn't see while I was in the experience. I lived inside the system every day, yet I couldn't see the patterns at play or their effects on me. You know how it works: you can't see the forest for the trees.

When you can't see or understand how all the pieces of the system align and work together, those pieces act as structural conflicts. These conflicts can keep you locked in the same place in the system, doing the same old things—you know, that "Same shit, different day" experience. If you are tired of the same old, same old, and if you are ready to find emotional balance to increase your personal and professional success, then EI$^{3.0}$ is the path for transforming into the next best version of yourself.

Emotional Balance

Using a feedback loop to diagram emotional intelligence reveals that it is influenced by emotional balance. This same feedback loop also reveals that the poles of emotional balance are true nature and the adapted identity; they are related opposites. The work of emotional balance is to return to true nature by disentangling from the adapted identity. These poles are explored in Chapter 5.

Emotional *imbalance* occurs when our bruised emotional imprints are in charge and dictate our responses to life circumstances. A person matures toward emotional balance, thereby increasing emotional intelligence and raising the EQ score by processing the bruises of the emotional imprints. Processing those bruises frees a person to optimize performance by responding favorably to life's ups and downs.

Achieving emotional balance looks like these specific behaviors:

- Not fighting even when the other is angry and trying to provoke a fight.
- No longer waiting to see how someone else feels before deciding how to feel.
- Realizing that being upset accomplishes nothing of value, and isn't worth the bother.
- Realizing that we spend more of our lives living with ourselves than with anyone else; therefore, it's important to be happy and comfortable being who we are.
- No longer using our emotional state to manipulate other people's behavior, or to punish them for past misbehavior— no more pouting.

- Not letting our life be a reflection of what's going on in someone else's life—each of us is in charge of our own lives with a distinct boundary between us.
- It means saying, "I'm going to have a good day today no matter what anyone else says or does."[20]

Your emotional balance is impacted by how bruised your emotional imprints are. In EI$^{3.0}$, emotional imprints don't contain emotions. These imprints contain feelings resulting from a foundational emotional experience. EI$^{3.0}$ diverges from other literature on emotional intelligence on this item. However, I reference the material of others who use the term "emotions." If you are reading a quote and see the word "emotions" in it, know that for EI$^{3.0,}$ it references feelings.

Foundational emotional experiences occur in infancy and childhood. These original events are fundamental to an imbalanced self-image. If the foundational emotional experience impacted your self-worth, then your bruised emotional imprint, when triggered, replays a story of *you're not lovable*. If the foundational emotional experience impacted your right to choose, your bruised emotional imprint, when triggered, plays a story of *you're not powerful*. These experiences of rejection are not mutually exclusive. It is possible to experience both.

Our undeveloped minds didn't have the skills or proper tools to process what was happening to us in those moments of harm to the self-image that included jumbled feelings. Without those processing abilities, our young minds interpreted the moment, assigning a meaning to the experience. The meanings we created out of those moments established the foundation for love and power in our lives.

These meanings are the starting point for emotional imbalance. They are internalized and hidden from view.

We stuffed down the associated feelings because we didn't know what else to do with them. The hidden meanings and the unprocessed feelings are the initial deposits in our internal emotional scrapheap. For many of us, me included, without a method for processing that original emotional scrapheap, it has continued to grow across our lives. More is offered on this scrapheap in Chapter 5.

The more the unwritten rule reinforces *I am not lovable* and *I am not powerful*, the more we act consistently with those meanings through habitual feelings and rote actions. As the unwritten rule and its enforcers continually fortify those original emotional experiences of rejection, it creates the ruts and grooves of the bruised emotional imprints.

The ruts and grooves represent a patterned whole-body experience of hidden meaning, habitual feeling, and rote action. As adults, we replay that foundational emotional experience about our self-image via the bruised emotional imprint whenever we have a similar experience of not feeling lovable or not feeling powerful, or when the *comfort zone* limits are activated. While we can feel our feelings and see our actions, the meaning is invisible. Bringing that hidden meaning into awareness can take years of working on ourselves. If the meanings and the feelings of the foundational emotional experiences remain unprocessed, the bruised emotional imprints of these misunderstandings can profoundly and negatively impact the self. Unfortunately, very few of us were adept at processing our emotional experiences in childhood, much less in adulthood. My perspective is not a judgment but an observation of the human system.

Processing and refining the bruises of an imprint requires five actions:

1. You must notice the rote actions of your habitual, unfelt feelings.
2. You must feel the unfelt feelings that are the trapped energy of the foundational emotional experience.
3. You must offer your feelings their rightful place in the system.
4. You must feel the story's hidden meaning.
5. You must recontextualize that meaning.

These processing actions usually don't happen simultaneously. They occur across time and are part of the dance of disentangling from the adapted identity captured in EI$^{3.0}$. These actions are revisited in later chapters, in discussions on the emotional openings that create the opportunity to refine and transform.

Transparency

Transparency felt important in the development of EI$^{3.0}$ because it is challenging to engage forces you can't see. These forces are conspicuous in EI$^{3.0}$. For instance, the organic development path from adapted identity to true nature is mapped end to end in The Model of Emotional Development. See Figure 4 for this map. It makes clear the nine leverage points that influence maturation toward emotional balance.

MODEL OF EMOTIONAL DEVELOPMENT

Unwritten Rule of Life: "It's not safe to be who I am (so I must be something else, and the system will dictate what that is)."

TRUE NATURE The

of the Made-Up Personality

EMOTIONAL STATE

INDICATORS	PROTECTION	EXPRESSION	INTEGRATION	SILENCE & ONENESS	PRESENCED WHOLENESS
		I am not lovable as I am Emotional Imprint			
Love	Absence of love/ Blind love	Blind love	Blind love/ Self-love	Unconditional love	Unconditional love with some imbalanced love mixed in/Whole love
Anger	Blind hatred/Hatred/ Focused hatred/ Focused anger	Focused anger/ Empowered anger	Inward anger/ Absence of anger	Completeness/ Perfection/ Is-ness	Is-ness with some imbalanced anger mixed in/Righteous anger
Release	*External:* Spewing violence aimed at all of life/Spewing violence aimed at one's life/ Spewing hostility aimed at a specific person or thing/Spewing demands aimed at a specific person or thing	*External:* Spewing demands aimed at a specific person or thing/Expressing empowerment *Internal:* Identifying as feelings	*External:* Expressing hopefulness/ Expressing harmony/ Expressing reverence *Internal:* Observing/ Integration of the past/ Honoring the past	*External:* Inaction *Internal:* Witnessing	*External:* Expression of balance with some imbalanced expression mixed in/ Expression of balance *Internal:* Occasional integration of the recent past/Integration of the present

	I am not powerful as I am Emotional Imprint				
Power	Blind choosing/Novice choosing	Empowered choosing	Empowered choosing/Intentional choosing	Choicelessness	Choicelessness with some imbalanced choosing mixed in/Balanced choosing
Resistance	Blind resistance/Focused resistance	Avoidance/Empowered resistance	Willingness/Acceptance/Revelation	Allowing	Allowing with some imbalanced allowing mixed in/Allowing and offering
Individuality	Blind individuality	Blind individuality/Empowered individuality	Empowered individuality/Adapted individuality/Integrated individuality	Communion/Oneness/Infinite	Infinite with some imbalanced individuality mixed in/Presenced individuality
Comfort Zone (The Boundaries of the Emotional Imprints)					
Energy	20 to 199	200 to 309	310 to 539	540 to 1000	*Humanity:* 500 *Divinity:* 600 to 1000
Awareness	Blind awareness/Some awareness	Some awareness	Awareness with some embodiment	Embodiment	Embodiment
Language	Life sucks/My Life sucks/I'm great	I'm great/We're great	We're great/Life's great	Silence, tears, and laughter	Silence, tears, and laughter with a mix of love, honor & respect/ Love, honor & respect

Figure 4. The Model of Emotional Development

INDICATORS

INDICATORS

ADAPTED IDENTITY The Inauthentic Expression

How these leverage points influence each other is discussed in Chapters 6–11.

Additionally, the bruised emotional imprints' hidden meanings and powerful defense mechanisms of anger and resistance are front and center. You don't have to spend years working on yourself to see them. You can also see the impact these imprints have on you in the form of the *comfort zone* and its indicators. By immediately normalizing these imprints and the impact they have, we appreciate how we developed the adapted identity with more compassion and kindness. It also allows us to see our true nature as a magical, creative ball of energy with infinite possibilities from the beginning, even if we don't believe in its truth yet.

The specific work required to mature through each state is also apparent. That work is identified and explained in Chapters 6–11. Doing this work allows you to partner with the forces that facilitate progress through each state and up the spiral of emotional balance. You don't have to figure out how to do the work, either. These forces, called dynamics, are leveraged in EI$^{3.0}$ using liberating structures. Such structures are designed to free the energy of those dynamics, enabling faster transformation. The liberating structures of EI$^{3.0}$ are identified in Chapter 13.

A final place of transparency is the ESI. The ESI measures, among other items, the maturity level of each of the nine indicators that are leverage points of emotional balance. Knowing the maturity level of each indicator reveals your emotional state. This state is your location in the spiral of emotional balance. By locating an individual's exact spot on the "map," we can see two essential aspects of emotional development. First, we can finally see the deep currents that lead us astray and hold us back. Second, it allows us to precisely point to the next best action to take, the step where even a tiny amount of energy applied will bring about a significant change. Thus, the ESI is a GPS designed to identify locations so that clear, concise, and meaningful steps can quickly be recognized and taken to develop toward emotional balance.

In the next chapter, additional greater processes of the universe that contribute to the transparency of $EI^{3.0}$ are identified and explained.

TOMI'S TAKEAWAYS from This Chapter

- $EI^{3.0}$ is the next advancement in the development of emotional intelligence.
- The feedback loop of systems thinking, with its structural conflicts and leverage points, allows the greater processes of the system of human endeavors to emerge.
- The beauty and effectiveness of $EI^{3.0}$ is its transparency.
- The big shift in development is to use the leverage points of emotional balance instead of the outputs of emotional intelligence for more effective and efficient transformation.
- Liberating structures free the energy of a system dynamic or leverage point.
- Emotional openings form when space is created in a moment that, if taken advantage of, allows you to see, know, or feel the world in a new way.

- For transformation to occur, a person experiencing an emotional opening must choose to do something different to leverage the opening.

- The meanings assigned to the various foundational emotional experiences that are the starting point for emotional imbalance are versions of *I am not lovable* and *I am not powerful*.

- These meanings are internalized and hidden from view.

- Bruised emotional imprints are a patterned, whole-body experience of hidden meaning, habitual feeling, and rote action.

- The hidden meaning and the habitual feeling of the bruised emotional imprints are the initial deposits in the emotional scrapheap.

Chapter Four

ORGANIZING PRINCIPLES

This chapter identifies the four organizing principles of EI$^{3.0}$ and explains the dynamics of each one. These four principles—system dynamics, spiral dynamics, creation dynamics, and energy dynamics—represent the greater processes at work in EI$^{3.0}$. They are the common threads that weave through the method, bringing it to life and determining how the parts and pieces interact. Additionally, these four greater processes are integral to the operation of The Model of Emotional Development. Their thumbprints are everywhere.

Why do I want to introduce these concepts at this point? Because not knowing how EI$^{3.0}$ is organized and not knowing how to use its organizing principles to your advantage are structural conflicts that hinder and delay movement toward emotional balance. As discussed in Chapter 3, to efficiently and effectively access all the potential in a particular system, we must identify the leverage points and structural conflicts. By doing so, we are able to unleash hidden potential.

Organizing Principle #1: System Dynamics

All systems must honor three mandates for the potential—and the performance of that potential—in the system to be maximized. These three mandates are order, belonging, and balance. Most of us aren't aware that these three mandates exist, much less understand how they work. Not knowing can be a problem. When we don't know the game's rules or how they apply, we can't play the game with grace, ease, and speed.

Let's start with the mandate of order. Order means that which comes first must be honored as first. Examples include the oldest child, the first step in manufacturing, and your oldest friend. Order also typically requires that we proceed in reverse order from how a thing was created to deconstruct it. This mandate is not absolute. We don't always have to honor order by going in reverse, as long as what we do doesn't dishonor it. There is a neutral space that is acceptable. In that neutrality is where the shortcut can rest (says the woman who loves shortcuts). For instance, typically, the interior elements are the last parts of a new building to be completed. However, when a building is being demolished, demolition crews don't work from the outside in. The fastest way to demolish a building is to strategically place dynamite around the foundation and detonate it. Since the whole building is being simultaneously demolished, there is no dishonoring of order. Shortcuts are acceptable as long as order is honored, or at least not dishonored, in the process. This concept of neutrality is also true for the other two mandates.

When deconstructing our bruised emotional imprints, order matters. The imprints developed from the inside out, creating a hard protective shell around our tender hearts. Due to such hardening, we usually can't look immediately at the foundational emotional experiences that made our beliefs about self-love and self-power. In the same way that the protective shell thickened layer by layer, it must be stripped away layer by layer. As we peel back the layers, we see more, know more, and feel more.

I am not saying that there aren't moments when ripping the bandage off and staring straight into the epicenter of your bruised emotional imprint isn't appropriate. Sometimes in life, it has to be that way for some people. For most of us, though, that isn't the way. The orderly and systematic approach is ideal.

The belonging mandate means that everything and everybody in a system gets to belong just as it is or as they are. To honor and comply with this requirement, we must allow people and experiences to exist in the system without wanting to change anything about them. When you seek to destroy, annihilate, get rid of, or exclude a person or an experience from your life, you are violating this principle. Resisting what is or what was dishonors the system mandate of belonging.

The last mandate is balance. Balance isn't about fair, just, right, or equal. It means an exchange of giving and receiving that serves the continued symmetry of a relationship or a system; it is about equilibrium. For example, it is typically impossible for a child to repay a parent. The child must go into the world and pay it forward by having children of their own or finding other balance mechanisms. Those mechanisms can include fostering a child, being a mentor, or being in service to your fellow humans in some capacity. It can also be as simple as a heartfelt tribute to your parents for their service to your development.

Another example is when someone gives you a gift, unexpected or not. Balance does not require that you buy that person a gift in exchange. Balance requires you to honor the energy that went into the process of giving you the gift (the thoughtfulness and the time). A verbal or written, heartfelt thank-you is a sufficient exchange that balances the system.

When these organizing mandates are dishonored or violated, the resulting imbalance in the system will begin speaking to you in the form of symptoms. Even though balance is a mandate, the result of dishonoring any of the mandates, balance included, is an imbalance in the system. Thus, balance is both a mandate and an outcome.

A symptom is a warning signal alerting you that something is out of balance. Symptoms can include ongoing family conflict, repeated injury, similar illnesses to other family members, repeated failed relationships, and repeated job loss, to name a few. If ignored, symptoms worsen and continue until the violation is resolved by restoring belonging, order, or balance. Resolution can also come in the form of the expiration of your human suit. That may be the only way to resolve the violation for some of us.

While EI³·⁰ relies on honoring all three mandates of systems, the principle that is typically violated by our personal experiences with *I am not lovable as I am* and *I am not powerful as I am* is belonging. In our quest for belonging, we relinquish pieces of who we are to the forces of the unwritten rule because we have learned that we don't get to belong just as we are. We need to be something else to belong, and we don't get to choose. If we try to belong in our unique way, we can find ourselves excluded from the system.

You have no doubt noticed that a big and bold paradox is happening here. Belonging to family and cultural systems just as you are is typically not allowed by those systems. Yet, those systems are supposedly organized around you getting to belong just as you are. What's going on here? What's happening is that most of us are living in systems that are out of balance because only a few of us get to belong just as we are. The enforcers of the unwritten rule are powerful and demand that we continue to show up a specific way, which keeps us locked in place.

Thus, we repeat the patterns of our bruised emotional imprints with similar results unless and until balance is restored. If you don't understand that your symptoms are connected to the dishonoring of a system mandate, then you will only treat the symptom. You will not see or solve the root cause of the symptom. If you do resolve a symptom without resolving the root cause, then new symptoms usually pop up somewhere else in your life until the root cause is finally resolved or your human suit expires.

If we attempt to behave differently from the system's demands, the consequences can be harsh, sometimes even catastrophic. If you wonder what that looks like and live in the United States, I offer Colin Kaepernick as an example. Recall his epic performance as quarterback for the San Francisco 49ers when he and his team won the Superbowl in February 2012. Years later, he was frozen out of the NFL by team owners because, instead of standing when the national anthem was played before a football game, Kaepernick kneeled as a peaceful protest to draw attention to police brutality and racial inequality. The ire and the backlash that this simple, peaceful protest received from the American public still reverberate years later. NFL team owners took away Kaepernick's right to belong. No football team would hire him. He lost his salary as a football player, which had to feel scary. Ultimately, he sued the NFL for blackballing him.

Another example from the United States is the treatment of former Federal Bureau of Investigation (FBI) agent Jane Turner. After Turner disclosed misconduct by fellow FBI agents in two separate matters of child rape cases and theft by FBI agents from Ground Zero, the FBI began downgrading her performance. Stephen M. Kohn, Turner's legal counsel, explained what happened to her:

> Jane Turner is an American hero. She refused to be silent when her co-agents committed misconduct in a child rape case. She refused to be silent when her co-agents stole properly [sic] from Ground Zero. She paid the price and lost her job. The jury did the right thing and insured that justice will take place in her case. For eight years the FBI misused its performance review and inspection process to justify vicious retaliation against an award-winning agent.[21]

Excluding those who don't follow the unwritten rule is a global behavior. Prince Harry and Megan Markle were pushed out of the royal family system in England for not playing the royal game the way the system demanded it be played. Once the couple announced they were stepping back from royal duties, the games began. They were stripped of their royal titles, stopped receiving protection for Prince Harry, and were shunned. At one point, Prince Harry's father, Charles, Prince of Wales, allegedly refused his son's telephone calls. Where is the balance in these behaviors?

To express your truth can be physically dangerous as well as emotionally painful. An extreme example is the Russian government sponsoring the poisoning of dissidents. The systemic message there is not only will you be punished if you speak out against the system; you will be erased from it entirely.

I have always appreciated and repeated the words of my friend and colleague, Shannon Schultz, on this topic: "We know what the system does to the truth-teller." Whether the demands are made by family, work, the city, state, or country in which we live, the Royal Family, government, collective conscious, or a football league, if we, as whistleblowers, speak the truth and are unwilling to play the game the way the unwritten rule demands it be played, we typically get excluded from the system in some manner.

Because the cost of opposing the systemic influences of family and culture can be so high, many of us dare not to do so. Who wants to be the black sheep, be ostracized, or maybe even erased from the system? I certainly didn't want that for myself.

Even if we dared to think about speaking out, most of us wouldn't know how to challenge, rise above, or break free from the unwritten rule without blowing up our lives. Few of us have been taught balanced ways for forging a path to our true nature in the face of these powerful systemic influences. It is no wonder it often seems easier to remain in a pattern of doing what is permitted. It's comfortable and safe.

But what if you don't want to do that anymore? What if the time has come to fully develop emotional balance so you can discover your true nature? The elements of EI$^{3.0}$ have been designed to facilitate balanced exchanges with the world from a place of love, honor, and respect. The method offers a balanced way to remove the cloak of the adapted identity so we can authentically express our unique personalities in the systems of our lives without fear of reprisal.

Organizing Principle #2: Spiral Dynamics

Emotional balance doesn't develop in a straight line; it progresses along a spiral. According to Dr. Clare Graves, the creator of the emergent cyclical theory of adult development that gave rise to spiral dynamics theory, "The psychology of the mature human being is an unfolding, emergent, oscillating spiraling process marked by progressive subordination of older, lower-order behavior systems to newer, higher-order systems as an individual's existential problems change."[22] The movements along the spiral occur on a continuum of development, from least developed to most developed. Transitioning through the different states in The Model of Emotional Development happens similarly.

Dr. Don Beck picked up the baton from his mentor, Dr. Graves, on this notion of development along an upward spiral, offering that "Each upward turn of the spiral marks the awakening of a more elaborate version on top of what already exists…"[23] According to Dr. Beck, these spirals reveal the "increasing complexity that exist within a person, a family, an organization, a culture, or a society."[24] The beauty of the spiral is that it honors belonging, order, and balance. First, inside the spiral, less-developed states nest within more mature states, honoring the mandate of belonging. You are all the states, even if you can't see or access the more mature ones yet.

Second, the spiral model honors the mandate of order. As you mature emotionally, you don't instantly teleport upward from one emotional state to another. Instead, you grow incrementally, one step at a time. That's a good thing. "Research has shown that of all forms of human motivation the most effective one is progress. Why? Because a small, concrete win creates momentum and affirms our faith in our further success."[25] These small wins also don't typically disturb the boundaries of the *comfort zone*, which can shut down growth when activated.

I'm not saying that giant leaps forward can't happen. They occasionally do happen. They just aren't the norm.

Finally, a spiral, specifically the Fibonacci spiral, honors balance through the golden ratio. The golden ratio is that sweet spot where perfect symmetry is achieved between two proportions, i.e., there is balance. Since this is not an arithmetic book, and I am not a mathematician, that is as far as our current conversation goes on spirals, golden ratios, and balance. Suffice it to say, because spirals honor all three system mandates, they offer an appropriate pattern for developing emotional balance.

Organizing Principle #3: Creation Dynamics

On the journey to true nature, we must shift from the powerless mindset to the mighty creator mindset. We *can* design the life of our dreams and then create it by consistently making choices that take us in the direction of those dreams. To do so, we must understand how creation operates and honor its process. Not understanding how creation works is a structural conflict that limits access to our potential.

Creation has two organizing mandates. The first mandate is a formula that invokes creation and invites the universe to take action on your thoughts to bring into the physical world what you desire. The second mandate is that creation has cycles. Typically, our appreciation for creation dynamics doesn't emerge until Integration.

Your creative abilities are freed through the liberating structure of the creation formula. To explain how this formula works, let's get all *sciencey* for a moment. Quantum physicists describe the creation formula as turning potentiality into actuality. As Dr. Hawkins puts it, "Potentiality is activated to actuality by the introduction of consciousness and intention."[26] For those who aren't quantum physicists, it can also be referred to as manifesting your choices in the physical world. As I understand it, when consciousness and intention collide, the wave function collapses, leading to emergence; in other words, what you desire shows up in the world. That means if you understand how to bring consciousness and intention together appropriately, what you choose (potential) manifests in the physical world (actuality).

The second organizing mandate of creation is that it has cycles. There is always a beginning, middle, and end to the cycle, which happens along a spiral.[27] This cycle applies to everything in the universe. It is why organizational change initiatives have a current state (the beginning), a transition state (the middle), and a future state (the end). Our emotional creations should align with this cycle, as well. There is an experience that triggers an emotional imprint (the beginning), feelings arise and are felt (the middle), and the feelings are released (the end).

It's essential to complete the cycle. When we don't feel our feelings to their natural end, creation stops, and we are left with the residue of incomplete creation cycles in which unprocessed feelings pile on top of what is already in our emotional scrapheap.

Relationship creation follows this cycle as well. Some relationships are intended for a short time, while some are meant to last your whole life. The trick is to know when to release the relationship. We humans don't tend to be very good at knowing. Still, when we hang onto relationships that served who we were yesterday rather than who we are today, we block new and perhaps better relationships from materializing.

The creation cycle unfolds at its own pace and in its own time, with some influence from us. Sometimes the middle lasts longer than you expect. Sometimes the end comes sooner than you anticipated. As we increase our emotional intelligence by maturing our emotional balance, we begin to recognize the cycles of our creations. We learn to appreciate where we are in the process and understand essential next steps.

Organizing Principle #4:
Energy Dynamics

Everything is energy. That includes you. Engineer and physicist Nikola Tesla knew this truth decades ago when he said, "If you want to find the secrets of the universe, think in terms of energy, frequency, and vibration."[28] If you want to leverage the secrets to creating the life of your dreams where effortless joy, unlimited abundance, and good health are your constant companions, then this notion that you are energy vibrating at a frequency all its own is a point of high-leverage change.

Energy is a multifaceted and complicated concept. I probably don't do it justice in this section, but we must start somewhere. It starts with getting all *sciencey* again:

Quantum physicists discovered that physical atoms are made up of vortices of energy that are constantly spinning and vibrating, each one radiating its own unique energy signature. Therefore, if we really want to observe ourselves and find out what we are, we are really beings of energy and vibration, radiating our own unique energy signature—this is fact and is what quantum physics has shown us time and time again. We are much more than what we perceive ourselves to be, and it's time we begin to see ourselves in that light.[29]

You and everything else in the world are energy calibrated to a specific frequency all your own.

Your mission, should you choose to accept it, is to play your unique note in the universe's symphony in the way that only you can. How does one find and play that signature note? Author Derek Rydall, the founder and creator of the law of emergence, offers, "The distance between you and your music is a distance of frequency." He observed, "The beat of abundance, the harmony of health, the rhythm of rich relationships—all the greatest hits are broadcasting right where you are." According to Rydall, the problem is that we cannot tap into the possibilities being broadcast right where we are. He writes, "This is a key reason we fail to fulfill our potential: our unconscious thoughts, feelings, words, and actions are moving in one vibrational direction while our soul is moving in another."[30]

In short, the low frequency emanating from your bruised emotional imprints keeps your human form cloaked in the adapted identity. It masks your high vibrating, true nature, or the frequency of your unique note.

What does this information mean for you? It means that your adapted identity vibrates at a frequency very different from the frequency of your true nature. The universe cannot align with the frequency of your true nature—the one that is busy vibrating at the frequency of effortless joy, unlimited abundance, and good health—because it is masked by the low vibration of your adapted identity.

The energy signature of your adapted identity comes from a dynamic equilibrium of the two energy signatures of your bruised emotional imprints. Unprocessed emotional imprints lower the frequency of your energy signature. In contrast, more processed and refined emotional imprints raise the frequency.

Each time you set an intention, the number of possibilities available in response to that intention is infinite. That is why it is called the field of infinite possibilities. The universe's response can range from horrible to magnificent to miraculous. What it selects from those possibilities aligns with your unique energy signature. The frequency of your intention draws to you an experience with a *like* frequency from the field. Thus, the internal frequency (your energy signature) is aligned with the external frequency (the energy signature of the circumstances the universe delivers to you). In short, you emit a frequency into the universe. That frequency attracts something of *like* frequency from the field of infinite possibilities. That is the Law of Resonance at work.

The Law of Resonance means you don't get what you think you deserve. Instead, you get what is aligned with the energy signature of your emotional imprints. You get what is required to notice patterns and hopefully become curious about them.

The Law of Resonance determines what materializes in your life. For instance, when you have a low-frequency energy signature, you don't attract people who can or will offer what you seek. What materializes resonates with the energy signature of your adapted identity, which seeks, finds, and draws a reflection of your emotional imprints into your life. In other words, what your life looks like on the exterior is a simple, uncomplicated reflection of what is happening in the interior.

As with the Law of Gravity, the Law of Resonance just works. You don't have to believe in it, but every day, just like gravity pulling you to the earth, resonance will pull to you similarly resonating people and events:

The Law of Resonance is the law which determines precisely WHAT IS attracted based on the resonance or the frequency of energy that is chosen by you through your emotional response system and as a result of that choice determines the kind and quality of the resonance or frequency projected which the Law of Attraction utilizes to determine precisely what IS attracted.

The simplest way to put it would be to say that The Law of Resonance is the law that assures that all energy continuously vibrates at a given frequency and depending on the vibratory out-put of this emitted frequency is what the Law of Attraction uses to determine what additional energies are attracted to one another which join together, resulting in a transmutation of the energy from the unseen or spiritual realm, producing outcomes in physical form.

To provide more clarity, the Law of Attraction will attract to you every event, condition and circumstance experienced in your life which is determined by the vibrational resonance created based on how you perceive what's going on around you.

The Law of Attraction makes no judgments, distinctions or determinations between what you might perceive to be good or bad, right or wrong, etc. and is TOTALLY unbiased in what is attracted to you. It only serves and acts as the delivery system, delivering to you precisely what you are asking for based on your resonance.

The Law of Resonance simply determines the vibrational intensity of what you choose to project which determines what you are asking for.[31]

I discovered one of the best explanations of energy and frequency, and how these ideas apply to humanity, in the pioneering work of Dr. Hawkins, particularly his Chart of Consciousness, also referred to as a Map of Consciousness.[32] See Table 1 for a modified version of this chart. Dr. Hawkins identifies the many levels of consciousness we can operate at as humans, associating each level with a calibrated energy frequency on a scale of 1 to 1,000, along with an associated emotion, process, and lifeview. EI[3.0] relies on elements of this chart to explain the evolution of emotional balance.

Let's explore the chart by first examining the opposite ends. The first level of human consciousness doesn't appear until 20, the calibration of shame. Shame's corresponding emotion is humiliation, and its related process is elimination. People whose lives are dominated by the emotion of shame have an energy signature of 20 and tend to be miserable in life. For this reason, shame researcher and author Brené Brown's work is extremely valuable; it helps people transcend the lower vibrations.

LEVEL	SCALE/ LOG	EMOTION	PROCESS	LIFE-VIEW
Enlightenment	700–1000	Ineffable	Pure Consciousness	Is
Peace	600	Bliss	Illumination	Perfect
Joy	540	Serenity	Transfiguration	Complete
Love	500	Reverence	Revelation	Benign
Reason	400	Understanding	Abstraction	Meaningful
Acceptance	350	Forgiveness	Transcendence	Harmonious
Willingness	310	Optimism	Intention	Hopeful
Neutrality	250	Trust	Release	Satisfactory
Courage	200	Affirmation	Empowerment	Feasible
Pride	175	Scorn	Inflation	Demanding
Anger	150	Hate	Aggression	Antagonistic
Desire	125	Craving	Enslavement	Disappointing
Fear	100	Anxiety	Withdrawal	Frightening
Grief	75	Regret	Despondency	Tragic
Apathy	50	Despair	Abdication	Hopeless
Guilt	30	Blame	Destruction	Evil
Shame	20	Humiliation	Elimination	Miserable

Table 1. Dr. David Hawkins's Chart of Consciousness.

Dr. Hawkins offered this information about the lower end of the scale:

In general, we can say that the lower end of the scale is associated with lower vibrational frequencies: lower energy, lower power, poorer life circumstances, poorer relationships, less abundance, less love, and poorer physical and emotional health. Because of the low energy, such needy people drain us on all levels. They tend to be avoided and find themselves surrounded by people on the same level (e.g., in jail).[33]

The Chart of Consciousness frequency scale tops out at 1,000, the level of enlightenment. Its corresponding emotion is ineffable, or beyond words, and its process is pure consciousness. And yet, we may be able to rise even higher on the scale. After building the Chart of Consciousness, Dr. Hawkins observed that a calibration level above 1,000 exists.[34] He called it the place of infinity. I believe that place exists, and in Chapter 11, I share more information about it.

Next, let's look at what occurs at 200, a frequency Dr. Hawkins considered the most important milestone on the chart. The level of courage, which happens at 200, aligns with the emotion of affirmation and the process of empowerment. This frequency represents the move from forcing life to happen to using personal power to create life. That shift is represented by gray shading in Table 1. It is important to note that energy signatures below 200 can be destructive of life both individually and socially.[35]

This dividing line at 200 is of similar importance in the development of emotional balance. Stepping into power occurs in the emotional state of Expression, when a person is courageous enough to take responsibility for their life by activating the power to choose. More detail is provided on this milestone in Chapter 8.

Next, let's bring the different elements of energy together. If your adapted identity is dominated by guilt, blame, and destruction, you calibrate at a frequency of 30 or close to 30, and you attract people and events into your life that calibrate at or around 30, too—people who feel guilty and destructive. If you predominantly live from the space of fear, which is filled with anxiety, withdrawal, and fright, then your energy signature calibrates at 100. That means you attract people and experiences that are also filled with anxiety and fear. If anger, hate, and aggression are your daily companions, as they were for me on occasion for a few years, you calibrate at a frequency of 150 or close to that, and you attract angry, aggressive people. And so on.

Part of the reason for sharing Dr. Hawkins's Chart of Consciousness is to show how negative feelings impact development and keep you locked in a pattern of attracting negative people and events into your life. The point is, if you don't raise your energy signature to a higher frequency, your life will be filled with the same old, same old. On the other hand, the higher the frequency of your energy signature, the more positive people and circumstances you'll attract into your life. "Your world simply mirrors your thoughts, your beliefs, and your expectations, like an echo in a canyon."[36]

If you are interested in further exploration of the Chart of Consciousness, I recommend reading one of these books by Dr. Hawkins: *Power vs. Force: The Hidden Determinants of Human Behavior; Letting Go: The Pathway of Surrender;* or *Transcending the Levels of Consciousness: The Stairway to Enlightenment.*

Increasing your energy signature to move toward emotional balance can bring you great rewards, but it is not simple to accomplish. While the adapted identity seeks equilibrium, you occasionally experience feelings from a higher or lower energy level. For instance, even if the energy signature of your adapted identity sits at a low frequency, you might briefly experience joy at the birth of your child or grandchild, or you might bask in the unconditional love of a dog. You can sometimes have a belly laugh at a good joke. These experiences can create a brief spike in frequency. However, the steady state of dynamic equilibrium is resistant to outside forces of change.

You can invite an energy shift in many ways, such as walking in beautiful surroundings, practicing yoga, exercising, playing music, or listening to music, whether it's opera, the sound of Himalayan singing bowls, or your favorite song on the radio. Singing, chanting, and drumming are excellent door openers. Your moment may arrive through education, either formal, such as a degree or certification, or informal, such as a podcast or book. One of my favorite energy shifters is laughter. Good belly laughs and tears of joy can transform and lighten the feel of any moment. The invitation relied on most in EI$^{3.0}$, though, is curiosity, as it is a liberating structure.

So let's get curious. What is your adapted identity and its bruised emotional imprints resonating with and attracting into your life? If life isn't mirroring effortless joy, unlimited abundance, and good health, then it's likely your bruises require processing and refining. Having the courage to mature emotionally allows you to shift your energy signature upward and draw more joy, abundance, and better health into your life through the Law of Resonance.

Connecting the Dots: Organizing Principles

There is tremendous power in appreciating the organizing principles of EI$^{3.0}$. When we honor belonging, order, and balance, we reduce the symptoms in our lives that limit how much we love ourselves and how much power we exercise. When we understand that development emerges along a spiral of increased complexity, we escalate our development toward emotional balance. When we understand how creation works, we can actualize the life of our dreams. When we understand that we are energy that attracts events and people of a similar energy signature, we are no longer ill-fated to live the default future where tomorrow will look like today. These organizing principles are the environment in which emotional balance matures.

TOMI'S TAKEAWAYS from This Chapter

- The greater processes at work in $EI^{3.0}$ are system dynamics, spiral dynamics, creation dynamics, and energy dynamics.

- System dynamics requires honoring order, belonging, and balance.

- Emotional development occurs along a spiral of increasing complexity.

- Creation has a beginning, middle, and end.

- You are energy emitting a frequency all your own—it's the note you came here to play in the symphony of the universe.

- What your life looks like on the exterior is a simple, uncomplicated reflection of what is happening on the interior.

- $EI^{3.0}$ is designed to align with and honor these greater processes.

THE NUTS AND BOLTS OF EI^{3.0}

Chapter Five

THE POLES OF EMOTIONAL BALANCE

True nature and adapted identity are opposite ends of the same spectrum. Discovering your true nature requires maturing toward Presenced Wholeness by accomplishing the work of the emotional state you are in and each successive state. Doing that work allows you to disentangle from the adapted identity.

The magic that happens in your life when you embody your true nature is vast. So, what is true nature? True nature is when your emotional imprints have been refined so they serve as guides and not guards. It is when you are emotionally balanced by fully loving all you are and choosing to use your unique talents for yourself and the greater good to create an amazing and bountiful life of balance. It is when your potential is in full bloom because you're authentically expressing your unique personality.

Standing in and operating from your true nature is the will of the universe, but many of us have moved so far away from our true nature across the arc of our lives that it can be hard to see from here. That's because the world sends each of us messages long before our arrival on the planet about who it expects us to be. These messages suppress and mask our true nature by telling us we are not lovable as we are, so we better be something else, and that we are not powerful as we are, so we don't get to choose. We learn we aren't worthy, that our voice doesn't matter, and that we have no control over who we are or how our lives will unfold. The unwritten rule teaches us that we are required to live in a specific space, and if we want to belong and stay safe, we must stay within those boundaries. Thus, separation from our true nature can begin before the doctor spanks us on the bottom, as we arrive in the world already viewing the universe through the lens of the unwritten rule.

I believe separation from our true nature happens because we don't have standardized methods or processes for operationalizing and actualizing our true nature. Our parents didn't know how to free themselves from their adapted identities, much less help us do it. I know mine didn't. Like all parents, mine did what they knew, and they loved me in the way they knew how. I love them for bringing me as far as they could and then setting me free, so I could go beyond what they knew. Hopefully, doing the work of discovering my true nature has afforded me the wisdom to untangle any of the elements of an adapted identity I helped create for my two sons during their formative years. A primary objective for me as a parent is for them to know their true nature.

This book offers a method for developing emotional balance so each of us can discover our true nature as magical, creative balls of energy with infinite possibilities. So each of us can be models for our families, friends, and the world on developing and using our emotional abilities for the greater good and our enjoyment. Yes, that is a lofty goal for our journey's end, but it begins with one step: gaining awareness of what might be masking true nature.

The Adapted Identity

The adapted identity masks true nature. The inputs of this identity are your distorted views on love and power that created the bruised emotional imprints of *I am not lovable as I am* and *I am not powerful as I am*. Thus, the adapted identity represents the adjustments you made to your self-image to abide by the unwritten rule. It is the inauthentic expression of the personality you were forced to make up. It's made up because it was who you *had to be* to stay safe and belong.

One of the most critical points to appreciate about the adapted identity is that just because it's made up doesn't mean it isn't real. Everything that happened to you is real for you. You also get to feel whatever you feel about the experiences that created the adapted identity.

Have you heard of the *Tabula Rasa* theory? This theory holds that humans are born as blank or clean slates. Then life proceeds to write all over that slate with its chalk, influencing the sense of self and teaching us who and what we are supposed to be. By now, you know what is written on most of our slates—the big unwritten rule of life: *It's not safe to be who I am (so I must be something else, and the system will dictate what that is)*. Unfortunately, nobody hands us an eraser so we can wipe the slate clean of that rule. The rule remains unspoken and unwritten, yet it directs our lives. I can't know to what extent you live by the unwritten rule, but I know I lived by it for years, and it didn't take me to the places I dared to dream about or hoped to go.

This unwritten rule of life seduces us into thinking these two thoughts about ourselves: *I am not lovable as I am* and *I am not powerful as I am*. These thoughts are the foundation for the adapted identity. They create bruised emotional imprints that reduce the size and potential of our lives by holding us in a *comfort zone*. These bruised emotional imprints make experiences seem very different than they really are. They contort our understanding to fit the life paradigm we have unknowingly and unwittingly accepted through enforcement of the unwritten rule.

Three forces grabbed the chalk out of your hands and wrote on your slate:

1. The childhood emotional experiences that teach
   I am not lovable as I am.
2. The requirements of belonging to your family that teach
   I am not powerful as I am.
3. The requirements of belonging to your culture that teach
   I am not powerful as I am.

These are called systemic influences. Whether people realize it or not, everyone experiences these systemic influences in varying degrees. By enforcing the unwritten rule, these systemic influences cocreate bruised emotional imprints that set the boundaries for your life by establishing a *comfort zone* around love and power.

Childhood Experiences

We learn about love from our family. The foundational emotional experiences that teach a child about love can be subtle or huge and overwhelmingly harsh. The overwhelmingly harsh ones can pierce the heart, breaking it in two, and even shattering it into a million pieces in some instances. The resulting hurt can be deep, pervasive, and profound. It can haunt a person their whole life, as it did my mother.

If your parents or the people who filled that role for you met your needs with love, warmth, and care, then your love imprint is likely balanced. How beautiful, and I am a little bit jealous.

The Family System

Our family system also influenced our sense of self as our respective families imposed their version of the unwritten rule on each of us. It means something different to belong to a farming family, a religious family, a family with roots in a foreign country, a wealthy family, a military family, a pro-union family, and so on. Meet the requirements of your family system, and you stay safe by remaining a member. Our desire to belong is so intense, we tend to abide by these requirements without being aware that they even exist, without ever challenging them, and without understanding the impact they have on our right to choose who we are and what our lives look like. Belonging can be comforting and satisfying but can also be costly and limiting.

The dynamics at play in family systems entangle us. Dr. James Hollis, an American Jungian psychoanalyst and author, offers meaningful insights into these entanglements. First, he reiterates Carl Jung's observation that

> the greatest burden the child must bear is the unlived life of the parent. That is, wherever the parent is stuck, the child will be similarly stuck and will spend his or her life seeking to overthrow such noxious stuckness, evolving an unconscious treatment plan whose purpose is to assuage the pain of the psychic burden of this static past.[37]

He also wonders, "What story, told or untold, threads its way through our DNA, our genetic coding, and plays out a same old, same old?"[38] In answering his own question, Dr. Hollis offers that

> the same passages, the same stupidities, the same delusions, the same inflations and deflations, and the same returns to earth play themselves out over and over. The past is not the past. The present is haunted by the archetypal dynamics which remind us that any story untold is an unconscious present. An unconscious present is a story which will insist on being told and will spill into our biographies.[39]

You may doubt that these untold stories, invisible energies, loyalties, and entanglements influence you. You may not believe in them at all. No matter; I'm here to tell you they still exist, and you are subject to their pull and their limiting forces.

The pull to belong to the family system is *so* strong that it inevitably affects the child. For example, a child will elect to be like the parent somehow, engaging in behaviors reflective of the family system, regardless of how much they say they don't want to be just like their parents. The pull of the family system will override their desires.

Rather than ask, "Am I subject to their forces?" it's useful to ask different questions, such as:

What has already been determined for us in our lives? When something in the past stands between us and our future, how can we allow it to recede into the background so that our view forward is not distorted by that past, but carried by it?[40]

The Force of Family Entanglements

Family entanglements are formidable. Looking at common entanglement patterns helps us to see how they are formed, and to possibly begin the processes of loosening their grip on our lives. Dr. Tarra Bates-Duford, a forensic psychologist specializing in familial dysfunction and traumatic experience, identified seven types of entanglements that arise from blind loyalty to the family:

- Accepting perceptions or views that are in stark contradiction to your own without questioning.
- Going along with a familial decision or behavior in order to avoid family conflict.
- Ignoring, minimizing, or pretending family issues do not exist.
- Failure to identify or acknowledge familial imperfections.
- Consciously transforming family issues into family virtues.
- Rejection of concrete examples of damaging family behaviors.
- Distorting family experiences to eliminate events that are unflattering to members.[41]

These loyalties are "blind" because we can abide by them without question:

> A family member that possesses blind family loyalty does so without hesitation or questioning of why they are supporting the family even when there are things that are concerning, in direct contradiction to how they feel, what they believe in, etc. Unfortunately, blind family loyalties typically occur unconsciously, unbeknownst to the follower, and done in an effort to maintain peace and homeostasis within the family. Sometimes, the blindly loyal family member will ignore or reject concrete examples of a family's damaging behaviors and actions in a deliberate attempt to avoid causing tension within the family.[42]

These loyalties can be challenged naturally in various ways. You can witness others model more mature behavior in a way that invites you to seek something different. The loyalty no longer aligns with your more mature self, so you release the loyalty. You can experience a moment so shocking that you must reconfigure your belief system, which causes you to release the loyalty. Finally, these loyalties can be challenged through a nurturing relationship like coaching, counseling, or mentoring, when the right tools are used to invite a shift.

There are gifts and limitations in these loyalties. As Dr. Bates-Duford observes, "Blind family loyalties can be both a benefit and a hindrance as blind loyalties can both build resiliency as well as keep us stuck in an ongoing cycle of dysfunction."[43]

These entanglements can determine what various aspects of your life look like, such as how long you live, your overall health, your finances, your education level, your love life, whether you get divorced one or more times, and on and on. Because these entangle-ments and their resulting hidden loyalties are so commanding, we often feel powerless to change our circumstances. We don't know how to exercise our right to choose something different and use our voice to express that choice in the world. Instead, we put our circum-stances down to fate when, in fact, our entanglements are making our choices for us.

Explaining with specificity how family systems work is beyond the scope of this book. My intent is to merely introduce you to this facet of the unwritten rule. Suppose you want to know more about how family system dynamics work. In that case, I encourage you to read one of the many books available on family dynamics and family dysfunction or to attend a workshop on the topic.

Cultural Systems

Finally, cultural systems have requirements for belonging, too. A cul-ture includes any system you belong to other than your family, like your place of work, your town or city, your state, your country, or the world. Cultural systems establish "the agreements a group shares about aesthetics, ethics, health, transcendental beliefs, power, rituals, and other beliefs that determine their collective identity."[44]

Does that sound like a familiar pattern? It should; culture is one more facet of the unwritten rule. Like family, culture nurtures partic-ular loyalties and patterns, entangling us in the system. As with family loyalties, these blind cultural loyalties can be disentangled naturally or through nurturing with the right tools.

Culture can be just as influential in our development as family can. For instance, consider how cultural influence can take away your power. If you don't think this has ever happened to you, consider your organizational life. Are you willingly turning your power over to an employer in return for money and security? Many of us do that. Author Carolyn Myss says we consistently make this bargain: "I will give up my talent and live in your shadow if you promise to take care of me."[45] That happens in far too many organizations and political parties as well. We trade peace for pay because it is the path of least resistance. We don't know how to act differently, and we need to put bread on the table.

The Effects of These Systemic Influences

Because many of us weren't taught how to feel our feelings or understand the deeper meaning of our foundational emotional experiences, they continue to pile up internally.

We carry around with us a huge reservoir of accumulated negative feelings, attitudes, and beliefs. The accumulated pressure makes us miserable and is the basis of many of our illnesses and problems. We are resigned to it and explain it away as the "human condition." We seek to escape from it in myriad ways. The average human life is spent trying to avoid and run from the inner turmoil of fear and the threat of misery...

We have become afraid of our inner feelings because they hold such a massive amount of negativity that we fear we would be overwhelmed by it if we were to take a deeper look. We have a fear of these feelings because we have no conscious mechanism by which to handle the feelings if we let them come up within ourselves.[46]

That huge reservoir is the emotional scrapheap. We cannot escape or avoid our feelings if we seek emotional balance. We must allow them to come up within us.

If bruised, our emotional imprints limit our ability to express authentically who and what we came here to be. Most of us have no idea these bruised emotional imprints are in control, setting invisible boundaries for how big we can be in our lives. They are invisible storage systems that

> preserve specific emotional learning—resentment at feeling treated unfairly, for instance, along with the corresponding range of acts that we have learned to be sensitive to, as well as how we have learned to react when we feel treated that way. These storage systems not only preserve what we have learned but continue to be added to by our experiences throughout life. These patterns lie dormant, waiting for a moment when something happens that brings the schema to mind. Then the old feelings, and the old responses, automatically recur.[47]

What makes those old feelings and old responses automatically recur is a trigger.

According to Dr. Margaret Paul, a bestselling author, relationship expert, and Inner Bonding® facilitator, we all have triggers:

> You know the feeling when someone makes a jokingly mean comment that might not be a huge deal to another person but totally destabilizes

you for the rest of the day? Suddenly, you find yourself feeling off-center and thrust into a bout of anxiety, guilt, or shame.

Sound familiar?

We all have emotional triggers. It can be challenging to identify what exactly those triggers are, but the process of getting to know and understand them can help us heal and learn how to cope better in response...

Why do we all have triggers? In short, because we were all children once. When we were growing up, we inevitably experienced pain or suffering that we could not acknowledge and/or deal with sufficiently at the time. So as adults, we typically become triggered by experiences that are reminiscent of these old painful feelings. As a result, we typically turn to a habitual or addictive way of trying to manage the painful feelings.[48]

In EI[3.0], the triggering event can be one of three things:

1. An experience in the present reminds you of a foundational emotional experience.
2. You've been invited to step outside the *comfort zone.*
3. You've stepped outside the *comfort zone.*

These events can bring a bruised emotional imprint to life, and it runs the show.

Because true nature is cloaked in the adapted identity, most of us pretend to be a version of an unlovable, powerless human being. I say most of us because some of you out there know with absolute certainty that you are a magical, creative ball of energy with infinite possibilities. No one and no event scribbled across that story on your slate. I celebrate you, but I am not one of those people. My slate was filled with *I am not lovable as I am* and *I am not powerful as I am* experiences. My voice was constantly drowned out by others telling me who I should be. My *comfort zone* was tiny.

Every day, I work on discovering my voice by accepting that all facets of me are worthy of love and by believing that I can create the life of my dreams. I am determined to express authentically my unique personality in a balanced way.

This work is seldom easy, though. In adulthood, the pain of trying to discern our true nature often seems too much to bear. Too often, we abandon who we came here to be and instead become what we think the world has told us we are: the adapted identity. We may find ourselves living in a small space, wondering, "Why don't I have a better life?" or "What else is possible for me?" or my personal favorite, "What the hell am I doing here?" That small space is our *comfort zone*. And we all have one.

The *Comfort Zone*

The *comfort zone* is the space the unwritten rule taught us it was okay to live in. This zone "is a psychological/emotional/behavioral construct that defines the routine of our daily life. Being in one's *comfort zone* implies familiarity, safety, and security. It describes the patterned world of our existence…"[49] The brilliant defense mechanisms of the adapted identity coupled with the systemic influences that enforce the unwritten rule work in tandem to hold the boundaries of the *comfort zone*. These boundaries are maintained and protected by the physiological process known as homeostasis. This process is typically hidden from you.

In physiology, homeostasis is

any self-regulating process by which biological systems tend to maintain stability while adjusting to conditions that are optimal for survival. If homeostasis is successful, life continues; if unsuccessful, disaster or death ensues. The stability attained is actually a dynamic equilibrium, in which continuous change occurs yet relatively uniform conditions prevail.

Any system in dynamic equilibrium tends to reach a steady state, a balance that resists outside forces of change. When such a system is disturbed, built-in regulatory devices respond to the departures to establish a new balance; such a process is one of feedback control. All processes of integration and coordination of function, whether mediated by electrical circuits or by nervous and hormonal systems, are examples of homeostatic regulation.[50]

Homeostasis goes on high alert when there is cognitive dissonance. "Cognitive dissonance is a theory in social psychology. It refers to the mental conflict that occurs when a person's behaviors and beliefs do not align. It may also happen when a person holds two beliefs that contradict one another."[51] This inconsistency creates internal discomfort and can activate the feelings of the adapted identity: anger and resistance. When we act upon these feelings, we have engaged our defense mechanisms. When confronted by life events that contradict our beliefs about the way the world works, we can either engage these mechanisms or shift our thinking.

The defense mechanisms of the adapted identity work hard to protect and maintain your *comfort zone*. And no wonder; that space is perceived as optimal for survival based on what the enforcers of the unwritten rule have taught you. The psychological process of homeostasis understandably thinks it will be disastrous or deadly for you to expand past this zone. It is this process that makes it difficult to take advantage of the emotional openings and dynamics that occur on the journey to emotional balance.

The forces that maintain your dynamic equilibrium won't easily be outwitted. Most of us are allowed to be only so powerful and only so self-loving before our bruised emotional imprints are activated, and out comes the parade of behaviors that keep us stuck in the same place. If you are about to travel past your *comfort zone*, the forces that maintain your dynamic equilibrium create all sorts of unnecessary diversions in your life to keep you in the zone of safety. Spiritual leader and author Howard Falco writes, "The ego, as the loyal protector and defender of your identity and existence, will use any trick in the book to keep you away from new truths, in the effort to keep you within your known comfort zone."[52]

Dr. Gay Hendricks, a psychologist, writer, and teacher in the fields of personal growth, relationships, and body intelligence, explains how these hidden, controlling forces can be invoked:

People often experience big breakthroughs… and then find a way to avoid relishing their achievement. They receive an award at work and then have a screaming argument with their spouse later that same night. They get the job of their dreams and then get sick; they win the lottery, then have an accident. The newfound success trips their Upper Limit switch, and they plummet back to the familiar setting they've grown used to.[53]

Why do the limiting messages we receive have so much power over us? Our lives are filled with rich and beautiful moments—witness the joy of a grandparent holding a newborn grandchild or the thrill of your first kiss—yet those magical moments don't make the same impression on us as the negative feedback we receive. Our brains hang onto "negative emotions like fear and sadness... These emotionally charged memories are preserved in greater detail than happy or more neutral memories, but they may also be subject to distortion."[54]

If we allow them, these forces can

twist our perceptions and bend our responses to suit their warped version of reality. They convince us that their twisted version of reality is how things actually are. They define our own view of who we have to be, and what is acceptable. In short, they keep us from displaying our natural flexibility, creativity, joy, and compassion by confining our lives along the arbitrary lines of thought, feeling, and reaction they lay out for us.[55]

We feel compelled to bend to the will of the unwritten rule telling us who we can be. We concede our worth and are stripped of our authority and individuality. We don't fight back because we don't even know what is happening. We typically have no idea that the *I am not lovable as I am* and *I am not powerful as I am* emotional imprints are the driving undercurrents of our lives, making them hard to confront and overcome.

Our brains aren't trying to play a cruel trick on us. They are trying to keep us safe by paying attention to and remembering those situations that threaten our well-being. This process is how we continue to survive. When a particular behavior threatens our right to belong to a system—and belonging means survival—we remember it and typically don't repeat it. Even when the behavior is no longer a threat to our right to belong, we may still avoid it because of the painful memories that arise. This type of avoidance pattern can negatively impact the development of emotional balance, because it keeps us playing small in a really big universe.

Why do we give up on ourselves, sacrificing who we are and what we were born to be and do? Relationship coach and author Dr. Susan Campbell writes:

> I am not alone in this game of limiting ourselves in the interests of staying safe. It is part of the human journey to start out whole, then to continually cut off parts of ourselves in response to real or imagined pain, and to spend the rest of our lives searching for what we have cut off, buried, and forgotten about.[56]

Teacher, author, and psychotherapist Tara Bennett-Goleman summarized this letting go of parts and pieces of ourselves similarly, using the term *schema* to represent the manifestation of the systemic influences on us:

> To some extent, our schemas embody ways we have given up part of what is possible for us. Abraham Maslow put it powerfully: "If the only way to maintain the self is to lose others, then the ordinary child will give up the self." Some schemas—and the ways we've learned to respond to them—represent a sense in which we've sacrificed our potential in a bargain to preserve connection.[57]

It's not just you. It's not just me. It's all of us. We all limit ourselves to preserve our right to be safe and belong. Think of a friend who is trapped in a loveless marriage or of a colleague forever failing to live up to the unattainable standards of their parent. We give up our self-worth, our unique voice, our right to choose, and our power to create for the reward of belonging.

We have a choice, though. We can spend the rest of our time on earth allowing our bruised emotional imprints to run our lives and keep us playing small in a really big universe, or we can discover the links that are holding us back, decouple from them, and spend our precious time on this planet being emotionally balanced. Maturing so you can be emotionally balanced is about freeing yourself from the bruised emotional imprints and subsequently expanding the limits of your *comfort zone*. Only then can you choose who you are, what you want your life to look like, and how to express yourself in the world without limitation.

I acknowledge that you might feel as if you have no choice. That's because the bruised emotional imprints that are written—and sometimes painfully etched—on our slates as we grow and develop are the antithesis of the universal truths of our true nature: **I am lovable as I am** and **I am powerful as I am**. Both statements are factual, but they may sound ridiculous to you, mainly because many of us are immediately immersed in an imbalanced form of love upon arriving in physical form. These experiences can convince us that we are not worthy. We don't believe wonderful people and magical experiences can show up in our lives with ease, grace, and speed, because we believe we aren't worthy of them. Alternatively, we can develop a bruise that gives us an inflated sense of self-worth, seeing ourselves more grandly than others do. Neither approach is balanced.

Similarly, upon arriving in physical form, many of us immediately experience an imbalanced perspective on power. We become convinced that we don't get to choose who we are and what our lives look like because we believe the system decides for us. We are taught to think we have no control over our lives. We succumb to the power of the system, and we yield our right to make choices, our right to use our voice to express those choices out in the world, and our power to create the life of our choosing. In the alternative, we can believe that we are far more powerful than we are, seeking to overcontrol our lives and the lives of others. Neither approach is balanced.

To choose differently, you can decide to discover the balanced versions of love and power where you love yourself and exercise your right to choose without the limits of the *comfort zone*. We can reclaim the parts and pieces we gave up in order to belong, by integrating the bruised emotional imprints of the adapted identity so that they inform and influence us from a place of love, honor, and respect, instead of from a place of pain, hurt, and limitation. As damaging as those imprints are, they are also incredibly valuable. The beautiful truth hiding within the adapted identity is that the unique personality we came here to express authentically is forged in the fires that created those bruised emotional imprints. We cannot be our true, whole selves without them.

What does wholeness look like? It is the place where we can access and use all our potential in a balanced manner. For me, it looks like living from the space of my true nature. I call it the state of Presenced Wholeness, in which we are emotionally balanced, where our most lovable and powerful selves are patiently waiting for us to show up, where joy, abundance, and good health are our constant companions. You don't have to be the Dalai Lama to experience Presenced Wholeness. The choice to pursue it is clearly and undeniably yours.

Most of us naturally mature toward emotional balance, though the journey isn't always intentional. Most people live most days with little insight into why they keep having the "Same shit, different day" experience of the *comfort zone*. Then one day, something big happens. It might be a cancer diagnosis, a car wreck where you experience life-threatening injuries, the death of a loved one, or your spouse walking in the house, announcing they are done, then promptly packing up and leaving. And you didn't see it coming. It is clearly and demonstrably an event that rearranges your life. There is life before this moment and then there is life after this moment. Out of such a pivotal moment arises the desperate question, "What do I do now?" These defining moments are the universe's way of shouting at us. They are designed to pierce the armor of the adapted identity to gain our attention so we can course-correct, steering our lives in a more robust and authentic direction.

Sometimes, we don't need a catastrophe to create a defining moment to transform our lives. We finally hear the whisper of the universe or feel its tap on our shoulder. It can look as simple as a moment of insight that shifts how we see the world. We transform our lives in alignment with the insight that occurred. It can also look like finally having enough life history to know that what we are doing isn't working. We walk in a new direction or blow up our lives to break free. Think midlife crisis or the uber-messy divorce. Both methods can look and be callous and unkind. Midlife crises usually occur around our fifties, or later for some of us, when we realize the choices we're making aren't taking us in the direction we want to go. Since society has taught very few of us how to disengage from the *comfort zone* in a balanced way, we do it in an imbalanced way that leaves pain and heartache in our wake.

We make it through the crises because we are resilient. We try one of two approaches as part of recovery: falling deeper into the adapted identity or seeking to break free of it. It may not be clear which path someone has chosen until after the fact. Then, you'll see a person who chose to mature out of the adapted identity begin to rearrange their life. Doing so can look like finding new friends, and leaving behind old friends; finding a new job, and leaving behind the old job; or possibly finding a new spouse, and leaving behind the old one. For the person who falls deeper into the adapted identity, you might see their hard shell become even harder through bitterness, resentment, disappointment, anger, or denial. These are beautiful protection mechanisms of the ego, and they can serve us well.

Once a person moves on from a defining moment, if they fell deeper into the adapted identity, they can remain in this new hardened shell until their human suit expires. It is also possible that curiosity about life has taken root, and the person will attempt to transcend and disentangle from the adapted identity as much as possible. They may ultimately drop off the radar to live a peaceful existence away from society. How this choice unfolds is explained in The Model of Emotional Development.

TOMI'S TAKEAWAYS from This Chapter

- True nature is using your unique talents for yourself and the greater good to create an amazing and bountiful life of balance.

- The adapted identity is the output of the many adjustments you made to your self-image to abide by the unwritten rule. It masks true nature.

- Childhood experiences, family systems, and cultural systems influence the sense of self.

- The internal pile of unprocessed emotional experiences and associated feelings create an emotional scrapheap.

- When a bruised emotional imprint is triggered, it takes over and runs the show.

- The defense mechanisms of the adapted identity hold the boundaries of the *comfort zone*, the space the unwritten rule taught us it was okay to live in.

- The beautiful truth hiding within the adapted identity is that the unique personality we came here to express authentically is forged in the fires that created those bruised emotional imprints. We cannot be our true, whole selves without them.

Chapter Six

INTRODUCTION TO THE MODEL OF EMOTIONAL DEVELOPMENT

The Model of Emotional Development is the centerpiece of EI³·⁰. It captures the action between the poles of adapted identity and true nature. Movement toward true nature is generated by the maturation of the nine leverage points of love, anger, release, power, resistance, individuality, energy, awareness, and language. See Figure 4 in Chapter 3 for how these leverage points align with the imprints, the *comfort zone*, and the state. Each of these leverage points is where a slight shift brings about a significant change.

The nine leverage points of the emotional imprints and the *comfort zone* are called *indicators* because they can be measured, indicating a person's level of emotional balance. These indicators mature along an organic development path, clumping together at specific points. Evolving these nine indicators toward balance is essential to freeing yourself from the *comfort zone* of your bruised emotional imprints.

Each indicator's organic development path is a sequence along a *continuum from imbalance to balance*. Thus, there are nine continuums in the model, one for each indicator. The natural clumping at the same points on the continuum for each indicator illuminates five specific maturity levels. These particular levels of maturity are called *states*. Thus, a state is a collection of all nine indicators at a particular level of maturity, i.e., at the same stage of development in the sequence from imbalanced to balanced. Each state contains only the sequence of an indicator that aligns with and occurs in that state.

There can be more than five sequences of maturation in an indicator's continuum, but there are only five emotional states. Accordingly, an emotional state might include two or more shades of an indicator. That is in keeping with the fact that creation cycles have a beginning, middle, and end, and that an indicator can be one thing at the beginning of a state and shift to something else by the end of it. Because The Model of Emotional Development is designed using leverage points that naturally hang together and continually affect each other over time, you can develop your emotional balance most effectively and efficiently. Follow the threads and you will arrive at the juncture of the balanced version of the nine indicators. This juncture is where emotional balance and true nature are achieved. You can fulfill your destiny and realize your potential here.

I believe there are few wonders in the world greater than witnessing someone showing up as the person they came here to be from a place of balance. In response to this authentic expression of the unique personality, the universe restacks itself, delivering effortless joy, unlimited abundance, and good health beyond your wildest dreams. It is a sacred moment. From this location, you will positively impact the world in extensive and significant ways and enjoy an unforgettable ride.

The Nine Indicators

The nine indicators in The Model of Emotional Development are influenced by the rule that *it's not safe to be who I am (so I must be something else, and the system will dictate what that is)* and its two resulting bruised emotional imprints. The three indicators of love, anger, and release make up the patterned response of the *I am not lovable as I am* emotional imprint. The three indicators of power, resistance, and individuality make up the patterned response of the *I am not powerful as I am* emotional imprint. Finally, the three indicators of energy, awareness, and language establish the boundaries for the *comfort zone*. All nine indicators are essential to developing emotional balance.

The *I Am Not Lovable as I Am* Emotional Imprint

As previously mentioned, three events can trigger the *I am not lovable as I am* imprint: an experience in the present that reminds you of a foundational emotional experience, you've been invited to step outside the *comfort zone*, or you've stepped outside the *comfort zone*. The bruised imprint is a defense mechanism protecting you from the pain of being unlovable. When triggered, our patterned response of hidden meaning, habitual feeling, and rote action takes over and dictates what we do next. The love indicator is the meaning, the anger indicator is the feeling, and the release indicator is the action. The extent that this emotional imprint governs us is determined by whether the bruise underneath the imprint is open and festering (so it guards) or processed and refined (so it guides).

The hidden meaning and the feelings of anger in the emotional scrapheap must be processed in order to refine the bruise of this emotional imprint and mature toward balance.

Love

The maturity of the love indicator reveals the hidden meaning of your personal story about love. Remember, it can take years of working on yourself to bring the meaning into awareness.

It is hard to see our worth when we don't love ourselves. It also makes it hard to love others because we can't give them something we don't have. Seeking balanced love is about learning to love yourself as you are and to value yourself simply because of your birth on this planet. Love, used from balance, can liberate you from the hurt and pain of any wrong or limitation. Only a few of us have experienced balanced love, though, so its restorative properties remain a mystery to many.

The world is filled with ideas and notions of love. I am curious. How did you consciously learn about love? One of my first memorable lessons about love came from a movie. As young girls, my sister Janie and I watched the 1954 classic movie *Brigadoon* with our father. In the film, the villagers in the Scottish village of Brigadoon want the village and its people to remain untouched by the rest of the world for all of eternity. To preserve the village, the village appears out of the mist of the woods in Scotland only one day every one hundred years. American Tommy Albright, played by actor Gene Kelly, happens to be visiting the day it appears. Over twenty-four hours, Tommy falls in love with Fiona, played by actress Cyd Charisse, a citizen of Brigadoon. At first, Tommy wants to stay in the village and disappear with Fiona. As the clock winds down, though, Tommy realizes he must return to America. He is not in the village when it disappears.

Back in America, Tommy realizes his mistake. He pines for Fiona and realizes he must return to where the village disappeared. He finds the spot, not expecting magic to strike again; after all, another hundred years have not passed. And yet, Brigadoon reappears. Tommy and Fiona are reunited because their love is strong enough to make it happen. The moral of the story, and what Dad wanted my sister and me to know, is that anything is possible with love.

> Love is the solution for all constricted or stagnant subtle energy and can instantly unlock all negative feelings and make energy free-flowing. Love heals all wounds, and quickly, when it is allowed to work. It is the most powerful energy of all in vibrational healing.[58]

That sentiment is true in EI$^{3.0}$, as long as we are talking about balanced love.

The type of love represented by the love indicator is not a waxing and waning sentimentality represented by falling in and out of love with someone or something. It is a state of being. It's a forgiving, nurturing, and supportive way of relating to the world. Love isn't intellectual and doesn't proceed from the mind; Love emanates from the heart. It has the capacity to lift others and accomplish great feats because of its purity of motive…

Love focuses on the goodness of life in all its expressions and augments that which is positive—it dissolves negativity by recontextualizing it, rather than by attacking it.[59]

We all aspire to such heights, but I must warn you that love is often one of the last bastions to surrender ground on the way to emotional balance because it has often been imbalanced for so long. I am not saying this to thwart your attempts to love yourself. I am merely sharing a difficulty you may encounter as you go about the work of emotional balance.

When this indicator is imbalanced, we constantly try to prove our significance by doing. We can point to our accomplishments as if to say, "Hey, see that? I did that. That makes me valuable and worthy of love." Part of maturing the love indicator is to stop seeking external validation that you are lovable. Doing so is an inside job.

Anger

The maturity of the anger indicator is a measure of the habitual *feeling* associated with the imprint of *I am not lovable as I am*. The more profound and deeper the hurt around not being lovable, the greater the scope of your anger. Seeking balance for this indicator is about noticing your anger and learning to appreciate how your anger signals that something is out of balance.

In its basic form, anger is "characterized by antagonism toward someone or something you feel has deliberately done you wrong."[60]

Because most of us don't have methods for processing our anger, it can build up and be directed toward anyone or anything, not just the someone or something that contributed to the original wrong.

As a child, every time you experienced a moment of not being lovable as you were, and you had nowhere to express the pain of that safely, you lost a piece of your self-worth. You also made up a story about what that meant about you. If you were like me, you didn't know what to do to keep that from happening or how to retrieve or reclaim that piece of yourself. Consequently, the experience created a bruise. As an adult, your anger reflects the hits your self-worth took as a child. It is also a vital affirmation of your self-worth.

It is important to stress this point: regardless of the origin of your anger, you are 110 percent entitled to it. You get to be angry about whatever happened to you. What you don't get to do is regularly dump your anger on your friends, family, coworkers, and the rest of the world. And yet that is exactly what many of us do because we don't know how to process our feelings. Rather than process internally, we release those feelings into the world. In our family, we call that the "Dump and Run." You dump your feelings in the laps of others, then you run away, so you don't have to be responsible for them. Our family has transformed to the point where the Dump and Run is no longer a welcome action. At least, that's true most of the time. As humans, sometimes we just have to let out what is inside!

Your anger is not only your right. It is an important messenger. As part of maturing toward emotional balance, your anger has to be noticed. Let me be clear: I'm not expecting you to do anything with your anger at this stage. Just notice it. Although many people think seeing anger means gaining control over it, it doesn't. A more balanced relationship with anger typically doesn't begin until Integration.

Release

The maturity of the release indicator is a measure of the rote action in response to the triggering of the *I am not lovable as I am* emotional imprint. When the imprint is triggered, and our emotional well is already filled with unprocessed feelings, our release actions are likely to have the full force of all the trapped emotional energy from the past behind them. We allow past feelings to dictate how we act in the current moment, and it usually isn't from a place of balance. That results in spewing through violent deeds and words.

As the release indicator matures toward balance, the trapped energy of the anger that feeds the release is processed so that actions can be sourced from the present moment without the pain of the past. The balanced release is a mix of internal and external action.

The *I Am Not Powerful as I Am* Emotional Imprint

When the *I am not powerful as I am* emotional imprint is triggered, our patterned response of hidden meaning, habitual feeling, and rote action takes over and dictates what we do next. The bruised imprint is a defense mechanism protecting you from the pain of being powerless.

The power indicator represents the meaning assigned to the experience; the resistance indicator is the feeling; and the individuality indicator is the action. The extent that this emotional imprint governs us is determined by whether the bruise underneath the imprint is open and festering (so it guards) or processed and refined (so it guides).

The hidden meaning and the feelings of resistance in the emotional scrapheap must be processed to refine the bruise of this emotional imprint and mature toward balance.

Power

The maturity of the power indicator reveals the hidden meaning of your personal story about power, which is your ability to choose who you get to be and what your life looks like. Remember, it can take years of working on yourself to bring the meaning into awareness.

Most people misunderstand power. They think it's about being right or getting their way with others or life. You can't always be right, and you can't always get your way. How your family and culture managed these power struggles and the conflict that arose from such scuffles taught you how to engage when being right or getting your way was at risk. It is interpreted as not getting to choose.

There are two layers to imbalanced power. The first layer is how you engage others when your power is challenged, i.e., being right or getting your way so you get to choose what you want. The second layer is how you engage life when life doesn't go the way you planned. It either proved you wrong or didn't allow you to choose what you wanted.

The Drama Triangle offers one of the best descriptions of how we engage others during a power struggle. The three roles of The Drama Triangle are Victim, Persecutor, and Rescuer.[61] While we can play each role, we have a favored position. This preferred position is referred to as the "Starting Gate," so there is a Starting Gate Victim, Stating Gate Persecutor, or Starting Gate Rescuer.[62] The Starting Gate is where we like to enter The Drama Triangle. These three drama roles are learned from the systemic influences of family and culture. When we are in these drama roles, we are blind to the fact that we choose to play a specific role in the triangle.

The Victim believes they can't take care of themselves and fears they won't make it in life. They feel like they have no power to change anything. The person playing this role is overwhelmed by hopelessness, helplessness, and powerlessness. The Persecutor is scared to look in the mirror and be truthful with themselves. Instead, they blindly choose to blame others and are in denial about their blame game. The person in this role doesn't understand how to take responsibility for their actions. Other qualities of this role include bullying, threatening, and dominating. The Rescuer's primary activities are to rescue others and fix whatever is wrong. The Rescuer will likely become bitter and disappointed by how much they have given with so little returned. The person in this role is waiting for someone to come along and rescue them. Instead of saving themselves, the Rescuer blindly chooses to rescue everyone else. Each role is a way to control the situation to claim power.

As for the second layer of power, we each have a version of The Book of Life. This book contains our lifeview and our understanding of how life should work. Most people's lifeview is some version of life's fair or it isn't. We make up rules about the way life works, and then we live by them, or our families pass down notions of life, and we are loyal to those notions. In knowing how life works, we feel like we have power over it and can know what will happen on a given day.

The Drama Triangle and The Book of Life are ways the systemic influences lock you in the *comfort zone*, so you feel powerless to change your circumstances. When you don't think you have any power, or that everything in life has been preselected, you give up your power to fate. In less mature emotional states, you might believe, consciously or subconsciously, that fate is in charge. When encountering things you cannot change, you may assume it means you cannot change anything at all:

Fate refers to the existential givens of life, those aspects of existence that are immutable, inexorable and inevitable, and over which we can exert little or no control. From an existential perspective, we are "thrown" into life without any choice or responsibility in the matter. We are born into a world at a biologically predetermined time, in a particular place, to specific parents, of a certain gender, and with innate strengths, talents, traits, temperament, limitations and vulnerabilities. All this is our fate, the cards we are dealt in life.[63]

Dr. Jung is said to have observed, "Until you make the unconscious conscious, it will direct your life and you will call it fate." In other words, until we recognize that our bruised emotional imprints are in charge, we will continue to think life is being done to us.

Upon incarnation, your soul accepts specific terms and conditions related to your parents, siblings, gender, race, and culture. Regardless of the state of emotional balance, fate will always be at play in your life in some form. That said, I also believe in destiny.

Destiny is what we do with fate, how we play the hand we're each dealt by fate. Destiny is determined not solely by fate, but by how we choose to respond to fate. We are responsible for those choices. Part of each person's fate includes a personal destiny. But whether that destiny is fulfilled or not depends in part on the person and whether he or she is willing to accept responsibility for and courageously pursue that destiny.[64]

The ultimate power of EI[3.0] and The Model of Emotional Development is that it provides a method for accepting responsibility for, and courageously pursuing, your destiny.

Author and psychologist Stephen Diamond offers the life of composer and musician Ludwig van Beethoven as an excellent example of the distinction between fate and destiny. Beethoven's youth was traumatic, and his young adulthood wasn't much better:

Frustrated by his unfortunate childhood circumstances and in his later efforts to earn a living as a musician and lead a "normal" life of marriage and family, young Beethoven became more and more angry and withdrawn from the world. Then, at twenty-eight, just as he started having success with his music, he began to lose his hearing. Such was his fate. His first reaction, understandably, was anger. Then, he fell into a deep depression. He laments in a letter that "the most beautiful years of my life must pass without accomplishing the promise of my talent and powers." Nonetheless, six months later, Beethoven decides "to rise superior to every obstacle," combatively refusing to submit to fate: "No! I cannot endure it. I will take Fate by the throat; it shall not wholly overcome me." (pp. 289–290) Taking this defiant stance, he turned his towering rage toward transcending the terrible tragedy of his eventually total deafness. Despite this awful fate, Beethoven went on to compose his most heroic and beautiful music, deterred only by death at the age of fifty-seven. There is a time to resolutely accept fate, and a time to furiously fight it. That responsibility is ours. Beethoven accepted his fate but refused to allow it to determine his destiny.[65]

Beethoven refused to be defined by his hearing loss. His response freed him from the trap of disability fate handed out. Instead, he aligned with and lived into his destiny.

Power isn't about being right or getting your way. It's not about surrendering to fate your right to choose, either. Power is about choosing to partner with infinity to create from your unique individuality. In doing so, your destiny is fulfilled. While that might not make sense now, as each state is explained and power is unraveled and rebuilt from a place of balance, the meaning of power will become clear.

Resistance

The maturity of the resistance indicator is a measure of the patterned *feeling* associated with the imprint of *I am not powerful as I am*. Seeking balance for this indicator requires learning to allow the moment to be as it is. Doing so honors belonging. The distance between resistance and its opposite of allowance is filled with the tension between how you think life should be and how it shows up.

Resistance is one of the most potent forces in the world, yet we are usually unaware of how it controls us:

Resistance of a psychological kind is, essentially, an unconscious unwillingness to open one's awareness to the inner truth that exposes our hidden participation in emotional and behavioral problems. Everyday people, even the smartest among us, can be limited to a surprising degree by their resistance to seeing and overcoming hidden weaknesses, while people with borderline and mental health disorders can be exceedingly resistant to knowledge and strategies that could help them become healthy.

Psychological resistance is an aspect of human nature that not only forms an inner barrier but also causes people to act against their best interests. Under the influence of such resistance, we decline to shift away from our negative emotions, to change our bad habits, to initiate plans and strategies for self-fulfillment, and to open our minds to more objective consideration of our perceptions and beliefs.[66]

Resistance keeps us from moving forward and encourages us to reinforce our limits. As Howard Falco writes, "The resistance you have toward any circumstance is a force of negative energy and actually helps in some way to keep the circumstance alive."[67] In other words, what you resist persists! This concept is crucial. Please allow me to restate it even if this comes across as a blinding flash of the obvious. Resisting a circumstance doesn't make it go away; resistance energizes the circumstance and makes it last longer. Thus, when you resist, you get the exact opposite of what you desire when you resist.

Author Michael Singer, in *The Surrender Experiment*, explains how we constantly stand in resistance:

Every day, we give precedence to our mind's thoughts over the reality unfolding before us. We regularly say things like, "It better not rain today because I'm going camping" or "I better get that raise because I really need the money." Notice that these bold claims about what should and shouldn't be happening are not based on scientific evidence; they're based solely on personal preferences made up in our minds. Without realizing it, we do this with everything in our lives—it's as though we actually believe that the world around us is supposed to manifest in accordance to our own likes and dislikes. If it doesn't, surely something is very wrong. This is an extremely difficult way to live, and it is the reason we feel that we are always struggling with life.[68]

Those preferences are determined by the drama role you play in the moment and the rules written in your version of The Book of Life. When life delivers something not aligned with those preferences, you can resist with all your might.

When the Victim is invited by life to take action on their circumstances, they resist making any choice. When the Persecutor is invited by life to take action on their circumstances, and they are confronted by the reality of not having the skills to take action, they resist by blaming others for their shortcomings and denying the reality of their failures. When the Rescuer is invited to take action on their circumstances, they resist their own needs in service of fixing the problems of others. Transcending the drama roles allows a person to stop resisting life in these powerless ways.

When my coaching clients say, "That's not fair!" I use one of my favorite coaching lines: "Can you please point to the page and paragraph in The Book of Life where it says life's fair?" Here is the news flash: The Book of Life doesn't exist. You resist life because it doesn't align with your preferences. When you get into a power struggle with the universe, the universe will win. Learning to allow the moment as it is allows you to engage life rather than resist it.

Resistance has acute implications because it violates the system-organizing principle of belonging. Whatever experience you are

resisting, whether it is one you have long denied or something aris-
ing in this very moment, your resistance is a message to the system
that your experience, as it unfolded, is unacceptable. It doesn't get to
belong. Those experiences may be uncomfortable or even painful, and
we may dislike or hate the feelings they bring up, but denying them
doesn't help us. It hurts us. When we don't allow people and expe-
riences to belong in the system just as they are, we create emotional
imbalance. Thus, we must learn new ways to engage our resistance to
develop emotional balance. When we are able to do so, the feelings
of resistance become a friendly messenger rather than a dreaded foe.

As an executive coach, it was sometimes challenging to work with
my clients' resistance. Just using the word resistance led to more
resistance. They could not look directly at the resistance. They had
developed a hard protective shell around their tender hearts—a shell
that usually only thickens with time. It's hard to get through that shell.

I should know. I find it challenging to work with my resistance.
When I was writing this section on resistance, I had to walk away from
the computer several times to allow my "resistance to resistance" to
subside. I'll need to purchase the special six-session package at my
counselor's office to unpack that one.

Resistance is tricky to spot. It's easy to confuse it with one of the
basic building blocks of life: contraction. Contraction itself is not a
problem. All of life flows from the natural process of expansion and
contraction. The contractions of our mothers define our entry into
life as they work to push us into this world (for most of us, anyway—
I have friends whose babies slid right out, and that didn't happen to
my children or me). It is one of nature's most beautiful examples of
balanced expansion and contraction.

Our breath cycles provide another example of nature's beautifully balanced expansion and contraction. Every minute of every day, we breathe in and out; consequently, we inherently know that contracting and expanding is life-giving. Resistance, however, is not about giving life; it takes a protective stance based on fear. Resistance, in other words, is an imbalanced version of contraction.

Contracting is a natural tightening in service of life, while resistance is a fearful shrinking not in service of life. The tightening of a contraction is an anticipation and a preparation for the expansion that comes next. In the constriction of resistance, we are withdrawing from the moment in fear, worried that what comes next will require us to change in some unwanted way.

When we get our lines crossed, which is easy to do, we can confuse contracting and resisting, thinking that resistance is important for sustaining life. Part of developing emotional balance is learning to discern what to resist, how to resist, and how to ultimately no longer resist.

Resistance is not all bad, of course. I can see the beauty and power in resistance as it transforms across its organic development path. It is the catalyst for the evolution of our individuality; this growth is essential for the refinement of the *I am not powerful as I am* emotional imprint.

Individuality

The maturity of the individuality indicator is a measure of the rote action in response to the triggering of the *I am not powerful as I am* emotional imprint. The enforcement of the unwritten rule results in the suppression of any individuality. To belong, we must surrender our individuality and play the role assigned to us by the unwritten rule.

Imbalanced individuality occurs when we are tightly in the grasp of the unwritten rule, doing exactly what the *comfort zone* will allow us to do. We are unaware of the right to sacred space for the self to blossom into who it came here to be. Moving toward balanced individuality requires the discovery of your unique personality.

There is a place in the world that only you can fill. No one else can fill it. There is something you have to do in the world. No one else can do it. At the intersection of these two items is your destiny. This filling and doing require you to peel back the layers of who you were *told* you are to discover who you *really* are—what makes you unique—and then build a life around your uniqueness. The journey requires exploring and claiming specific elements of your individuality and evolving your lifeview.

The *Comfort Zone*

The *comfort zone* is established by the boundaries around love and power that are created by the unwritten rule and honored by emotional imprints. As a reminder, its job is to keep you from stepping outside the invisible fence established by your version of the unwritten rule. As with the emotional imprints, there are three indicators for the *comfort zone*: energy, awareness, and language.

These three indicators work together to control how and when new insights about emotional development occur that allow you to mature. Understanding how they work is integral to taking advantage of the opportunities to see yourself and the world in new ways. However, you might not recognize such openings, or if you do notice them, you may not understand what they offer. That's because you are part of the lacework of the system yourself, and as such, there are some insights you can't access until after the fact.

Let's unpack that. When you play your role in a system, it can be tough to see the patterns at play or their effect on you because you are part of the pattern. You are so well integrated, you don't even know that there is a pattern, much less how to do something different.

Thus, you may be blind to the next step; you may not even know that there *is* a next step. As long as you wear these blindfolds, you are destined to repeat the same patterns of detrimental behavior. I know this pattern has been true for me; many of my readiness paths were invisible to me until I reached more emotionally balanced levels.

I'm willing to bet your experience is similar. Even though the balanced version of all the indicators referenced in this chapter is available to you at every moment, you aren't aware of it because it is not within the scope of awareness for your level of emotional balance. You're not at fault in any way; we all see what we are prepared to see. Nothing more; nothing less. As German philosopher Arthur Schopenhauer said, "Every man takes the limits of his own field of vision for the limits of the world."[69]

This blindness is one of the most brilliant protection mechanisms of the human system—and it also holds you back. To move forward, you must leverage these emotional openings. Taking advantage of them is essential to developing emotional balance.

Energy

The maturity of the energy indicator represents the combined frequency of both emotional imprints. That frequency is determined by the amount of pain and hurt your bruises contain. This frequency is your energy signature, and it operates as the energetic set point for your life.

Spiral development teaches that everything exists in every moment inside the spiral. Still, you can usually only be aware of what the boundaries of your *comfort zone* permit you to understand. However, an emotional opening creates an opportunity for you to experience something outside the *comfort zone*. In the early stages of emotional balance, that something is usually an increased energy frequency created by a forced, defining moment. If you can take advantage of the different frequencies available in an emotional opening to expand the *comfort zone*, it is an opportunity to experience a more balanced space. In some instances, a lower-energy frequency with harsher feelings can be revisited during an emotional opening. There are no guarantees that you will take advantage of the energy spike or that you will get stuck in the energy drop, and both are possible. More detail is provided on the energy signature and emotional openings in the description of each state in the following five chapters.

New insights and revelations float by you all the time. The challenge is that you typically aren't at an energy signature that allows you to notice these subtle energy spikes and their messages about the world and your place in it. It is why maturing your energy signature is key to expanding your *comfort zone*.

In keeping with the creation mandates, the energy range in each emotional state has a beginning, middle, and end. The lower-energy frequency is associated with the beginning of that state and the higher-energy frequency with the end of that state. It isn't a perfect science, as there are few absolutes in the world. Thus, each state's energy range is an estimate based on my observations and influenced by the Chart of Consciousness.

Awareness

The maturity of the awareness indicator is a measure of the awareness you possess about yourself and your surroundings. Awareness is

> a capacity of the human mind. As we ordinarily understand it, it's the ability to directly know and to perceive, sense, feel, or be cognizant of experience. We might think of awareness simply as the state of being conscious of something.[70]

In The Model of Emotional Development, awareness takes two forms. You may not be aware, or you are aware through seeing, knowing, or feeling. Not being aware is blind awareness, and it is the least balanced level of awareness. Feeling, known as embodiment, is the most balanced level of awareness. Typically, embodiment is not available to a person until Integration.

Embodiment is the art of being connected to your body and relying on its wisdom. It's a total body approach to life. It's balanced, using heart and head. Somatic/Body Therapist Barbara Nordstrom-Loeb explains this whole-body approach to knowing and describes how we sacrifice it by relying only on our minds:

> From the moment we are born our bodies are essential to our learning, growth and relationships with others. Throughout our lives, our bodies and movements communicate much more clearly than our words. As an educator, psychotherapist and healer, I am continually awed by

the wisdom that results from listening and paying attention to our bodies' wisdom.

For most of us today, disconnecting from our bodies and movement might feel like the only option available to us. We privilege our thoughts and minds, without being curious about their relationship to the rest of who we are. Doing this, we end up feeling out of balance with our community, our world, and ourselves.[71]

If you have shut down your body to feeling, you can reconnect as you develop emotional balance. Embodying requires you to open your heart and feel what you know.

If the foundational emotional experience impacted love, your system froze your heart through numbness as an act of self-preservation. If that is true for you, you struggle with embodied awareness. Some events pierce the numbness, such as the birth of a child, the love of a pet, the death of a loved one, or the birth of a grandchild, but those experiences of embodied awareness by the heart are few and far between.

Experiencing a catastrophic trauma that overwhelms the heart can completely shut it down, so a person feels nothing at all. An example might be a child who experiences war or a soldier who experiences active combat. In order to protect the self from the mercilessness and unforgiving nature of war, the heart shuts down. A person may describe this shutdown as "just going through the motions," or being totally disconnected from life. Even though the effects of this type of trauma can be understood through the lens of EI$^{3.0}$, treatment of this type of experience requires a specifically trained healthcare professional and is beyond the scope of EI$^{3.0}$.

If the foundational emotional experience impacted power, your system froze an image into your mind of who you are and what the world is as an act of self-preservation. If that is true for you, you experience resistance that limits the ability to see and know. There are certain events that are powerful enough to pierce the resistance but those are few and far between.

Experiencing a catastrophic trauma that overwhelms the mind such as a natural disaster, the tragedies of war, or a violent crime can completely shut down the mind. This shut down reveals itself in catatonic behaviors like immobility (certain body parts or the whole body), muteness, or inability to mentally process (blankness). Even though the effects of this type of experience can be understood through the lens of EI$^{3.0}$, treatment of this type of harm to the self-image requires a specifically trained healthcare professional and is beyond the scope of EI$^{3.0}$.

Solely encountering new knowledge is not enough to create transformation, as "recognizing something new does not necessarily lead to acting differently."[72] After all, we receive new information all the time and fail to change our ways.

The missing ingredient in this encounter is curiosity. Curiosity allows a person to take advantage of a spike in energy and the opening for awareness. The liberating structure of curiosity, as Celeste Kidd and Benjamin Y. Haden write, "is a basic element of our cognition, yet its biological function, mechanisms, and neural underpinning remain poorly understood."[73]

Definitions of curiosity range from the simple to the complex. I find that a simple definition meets the needs of EI$^{3.0}$. Curiosity, according to Kidd and Haden, is "a special form of information-seeking distinguished by the fact that it is internally motivated."[74] Curiosity "enhances learning, consistent with the theory that the primary function of curiosity is to facilitate learning."[75] Curiosity is essential to developing emotional balance, because it invites people to focus their effort on useful information that they do not yet possess, like why they might be angry or resistant. Yet, I did not designate curiosity as an indicator because it is a liberating structure that frees the power of the indicators of energy and awareness. Additionally, my observations of curiosity did not reveal levels of maturity as did the nine indicators.

Curiosity is activated by asking questions. Yet, most of us don't ask questions to broaden our world. We ask a question because we want a particular answer or the "right" answer. Ironically, looking for answers traps us. Questions, however, are "more transformative than answers and are the essential tools of engagement...if you want to change the context, find powerful questions."[76] We can use questions to enlarge the conversation we have with life because "questions create the space for something new to emerge."[77] According to Romanian-French Playwright Eugene Ionesco, "It is not the answer that enlightens, but the question."[78] The larger the question is, the larger the conversation. The larger the conversation is, the larger the life.

Curiosity must be *internally motivated* to open us to new ideas. It must always be the individual's choice to pursue information. As a coach, you needn't provide all the answers. Instead, you can invite curiosity by saying, "I am curious about that. Can you tell me more?" Such an inquiry might evoke deeper thought and reflection. Such reflection invites the person to pursue a deeper meaning. This kind of self-inquiry leads to deeper, longer-lasting learning as it "may further benefit the learner by enhancing the encoding and retention of the new information."[79] Thus, the deeper we can invite someone to go within through the doorway of curiosity, the greater the possibility for an insight that will offer a path of transformation.

Language

The language indicator is how a person articulates the *comfort zone*. The language used can put a new lens on behavior, influencing how we and others interpret the world.[80]

> Speaking, writing and reading are integral to everyday life, where language is the primary tool for expression and communication. Studying how people use language—what words and phrases they unconsciously choose and combine—can help us better understand ourselves and why we behave the way we do.[81]

While we create our reality with our language, most of us aren't aware that we are even doing so. "When a person looks out at the world, he sees it filtered through a screen of his words, and this process is as invisible to him as water is to fish."[82] In short, building our reality is invisible to most of us. We can only make the process visible by understanding the maturity level and meaning of the language we use.

One of the most detailed descriptions of the stages of human language comes from the work of Dave Logan, John King, and Halee Fischer-Wright. This trio studied organizations and discovered that they are tribal in nature. A tribe is "any group of people between about 20 and 150 who know each other enough that, if they saw each other walking down the street, would stop and say 'hello.'"[83] The researchers also learned that there are five languages that different tribes speak:

- Stage One is "Life sucks." About 2 percent of tribes are at this stage. It produces people who do horrible things—a culture of gangs and prisons.[84]
- Stage Two is "My life sucks." About 25 percent of tribes are at this stage. It is represented by despairing hostility and doing whatever it takes to survive.
- Stage Three is "I'm great." About 48 percent of tribes are at this stage. Inherent in "I am great" is that you are not.
- Stage Four is "We're great." About 22 percent of tribes are at this stage. Here, people are oriented by their values—united by something greater than individual needs and wants.
- Stage Five is "Life's great." About 2 percent of tribes are at this stage, and they change the world.

These stages are mainly invisible to us. "Without any external coaching, people advance through stages very slowly."[85] Tell me about it. Stage Two and Stage Three are longtime friends of mine.

Movement is slow because tribes and their individual members can hear only one stage above and below the current stage of the language they speak.[86] Thus, a person at the level of "Life sucks" likely will not be able to hear a person speaking the language of "I'm great!" Similarly, hearing the language of "Life's great" that is spoken in Integration is beyond what a person in Protection speaking the language of "Life sucks" can hear.

While Logan, King, and Fischer-Wright made their discoveries working with organizations, the tribal languages they identified are a meta version of how individuals in the tribe speak. In short, the language of the whole is made up of the majority of the individual members' spoken language. For me, these five stages make perfect sense as indicators of the emotional state of individuals in Protection, Expression, and Integration, which includes about 99 percent of the adult population.

Given that only a tiny percentage of the world's population is in the last two emotional states of Silence & Oneness and Presenced Wholeness, I suspect Stage Six and Stage Seven didn't show up in the research of Logan, King, and Fischer-Wright. Since the languages identified by their model cover only the first three emotional states in $EI^{3.0}$, I expanded it by adding Stage Six and Stage Seven to cover the last two emotional states. The language that represents Stage Six is a language of silence, tears, and laughter, indicative of witnessing and oneness. The bruises of the emotional imprints have been integrated and refined, so no inner turmoil or interference needs to be verbalized.

When it is necessary to speak, the language that aligns with Stage Seven is one of love, honor, and respect. The person in this stage engages in interactions with others who seek to create, maintain, or advance system balance.

While all nine indicators are essential to determining emotional balance, language can be a simplified diagnostic tool for estimating someone's location in the development spiral. Language holds a unique position among the indicators because it is the verbal presentation of the emotional scrapheap. If you use language as a diagnostic tool to assess emotional balance, remember that people are never just one-dimensional. Understanding the stage of language spoken is a starting point, not a definitive answer.

General Features of Indicators

It is essential to know some general features about the nine indicators, such as their propensity for crisscrossing and regularly pinging off each other. Even though each indicator follows its own organic development path across a continuum, they continually interact with and influence each other. The Model of Emotional Development captures the continuums I saw for each indicator as I matured toward emotional balance. The nuances of your journey may be slightly different, or vastly different, but the model provides a basic map and a language for what is taking place.

I freely admit that there may be more than nine indicators that are relevant to emotional balance. Still, the indicators selected for The Model of Emotional Development are the ones that, when matured, result in high-leverage change. I think our time is best spent focusing on those leverage points that will move us toward our true nature more efficiently and effectively.

A Word on My Process

The organic development path that revealed itself for the indicators represents and honors orderly maturation, internally and externally. Leaps of faith are no longer required. You know what the map and your next steps look like because you can see the order in which events unfold. A word of caution as you proceed: even though the organic development path for each indicator is depicted in Figure 4 as evolving along a continuum, maturation still happens in a spiral. Don't let the continuum concept draw you too far into linear thinking.

That said, here is how I envision the continuums. Each indicator's continuum honors belonging, order, and balance. Because they house the complete maturation cycle from imbalanced to balanced, they allow all phases of an indicator to belong just as they are. None of the conduct included in a continuum is good or bad, although we may label it as such because of the harm an action may inflict on the self or others. My primary goal in using the selected labels was to represent balance or imbalance.

You should also be aware that I designated labels and created descriptions of sequencing patterns after living through them. In the middle of a transformation, I might not have had words for what was taking place, or I might not have understood the experience until I was on the other side of it. For instance, in Expression, I use the word boundaries to describe the fences people build to protect themselves even though most people in Expression do not use that word. Instead, they might say they are drawing lines in the sand that they don't want to be crossed. They know their boundaries are being violated, but they don't have the words for it yet. Thus, you may not describe your experiences the same way I do here, though I believe the underlying themes will be similar. Soon enough, we will share a common vocabulary.

I also feel compelled to note that, in some instances, my description of what occurs across an indicator or in a state is wholly inadequate. I have done my best to find the right words to explain what takes place as one emotionally matures, but there are moments when human words cannot capture the experience.

I appreciate and value how author David Kessler summarizes his work with author Elisabeth Kübler-Ross on the five states of grief. What he wrote parallels how I feel about EI$^{3.0}$:

The five stages were never intended to be prescriptive... They don't prescribe, they describe. And they describe only a general process. Each person grieves in their own unique way. Nonetheless, the grieving process does tend to unfold in stages similar to what we described, and most people who have gone through it will recognize them.[87]

EI[3.0] is not intended to be prescriptive. It describes a general process that each of us will travel through in our unique way as we seek emotional balance.

I also did not intend for any indicator to determine a person's emotional state, although the language indicator is a starting point if you have no other available tools. While each indicator is significant, I reiterate that people are never just one-dimensional. We want to capture an emotional snapshot of the entire person. That is why the ESI measures the maturity of all indicators. Accordingly, I advise you to use as many indicators as possible to decide about emotional balance. You can leverage the information you uncover to create meaningful and appropriate growth opportunities for you and your clients.

As you reflect on what you learn during this journey, remember that it is best not to judge yourself or anyone else. We are all doing the best we can based on what we know. The more you know, the better you can do. The better you do, the more you inspire others to do the same.

Those are not just pretty words—I have experienced some beautiful halo effects from my efforts to develop emotional balance. As I gained insights into myself, I applied those insights to others. It changed how I interacted with them, and allowed compassion, empathy, grace, forgiveness, and optimism to develop naturally. $EI^{3.0}$ doesn't focus on the specific elements of emotional intelligence for just this reason—those outcomes naturally occur as one matures emotionally. And because you can more readily offer others what you have for yourself and give to yourself, you can pass these gifts on to others.

Last but not least, don't stop laughing. Some days the only thing that saved me from the horrible guilt and shame I had about my past behavior was laughter. I would look at the mess I made, laugh, and remind myself that if I had the power to create such a disaster by accident, I had the power to create something genuinely magnificent when I tried.

The Natural Maturation Process for Indicators

Suppose a person can capitalize on an emotional opening to increase their energy signature or become aware of something new. In that case, other indicators can also mature, thereby refining emotional imprints and expanding the *comfort zone*. These openings are defining moments that can be forced or natural.

A forced defining moment is when the universe intervenes with a life-changing event that is strong enough to interrupt the ruts and grooves of the emotional imprints. As I mentioned previously, it is the universe's way of shouting at us. The moment of turmoil and turbulence demands transformation and maturation. Even though it is demanded, we may not be able to open ourselves up to the moment enough to take advantage of the invitation. A natural defining moment is when the ordinary dynamics of emotional development are leveraged across time to facilitate transformation and maturation. This defining moment via a less confrontational invitation is most likely a moment of insight or revelation that occurs in due course along the organic path of maturation. At this moment, the universe is either tapping us on the shoulder or whispering in our ear. Just like a forced defining moment, we can also choose to ignore the natural defining moment. Regardless of the type of opening, it is always your choice to transform.

Both types of openings can be nurtured when an individual—such as a coach, counselor, leader, or mentor—or a group facilitates a person's transition into the next-larger system.

I can't emphasize enough how crucial these openings are, yet they can be hard to use to good advantage, especially if you don't understand what is happening or have the means to leverage the moment. However, one of the beautiful aspects of The Model of Emotional Development is that these openings are identified and explained, making them easier to leverage.

In the emotional state of Protection, especially in the beginning and middle, openings usually have to be forced. Force is necessary because our protection mechanisms in this state are remarkable. The shield built by the human system to protect the heart is as challenging for you to break through as a spider web is to a fly. It is a magnificent and monstrous defense system, sheltering us from the profoundly damaging experiences that created our emotional imprints.

In more mature states, the emotional opening is likely to occur naturally across time. As we mature toward emotional balance, different elements come into view at different times. The work can feel tedious, like you're clearing land overgrown with brush. You are busy looking down, chopping and clearing, working hard to forge a new path through the brush, but you can't see very far ahead of yourself as you go. As some of the brush is cleared, i.e., specific indicators mature, you can see more landscape. You look up to see beautiful things you never noticed before because the debris had been in the way. Now, space for reflection becomes available to you. Rinse and repeat as long as it takes to achieve emotional balance.

Evolving toward emotional balance takes time because there is almost always a processing period in the wake of insight or revelation from an emotional opening. It takes a period of percolation and fermentation to process the new information and use it to expand the prescribed *comfort zone*. As this new information permeates the different aspects of our lives over time, we can implement what we have learned. Take the time, and you will be rewarded.

Time spent processing before moving into a new beginning, middle, or end is time well spent. It allows you to deepen into what took place. That deepening in the wake of an insight precipitates small, incremental shifts that you may not even notice until one day everything is different.

The percolating period lasts as long as it lasts. Still, we do have some clues as to duration on maturing indicators from the field of personal development. "Most people see measurable, enduring changes three to six months after they begin working on a skill."[88] While you aren't technically practicing a new skill, you are learning something new about yourself and how to use that information to show up in the world in a new way. One of the best things you can do is be patient and give yourself three to six months to see the rewards of your efforts to evolve toward emotional balance.

Before you begin your journey, you should also know that not all indicators develop at the same pace. For instance, a person may have a specific value or strength that allows them to excel in one indicator but not others. It is also possible that one imprint has been refined and the other one hasn't.

Maybe you've heard of the artist whose work is world-renowned, but their love life is a train wreck? That profile reflects someone whose *I am not powerful as I am* imprint is more mature than their *I am not lovable as I am* imprint. Another example is someone whose love for themselves and others is unconditional, but they can't quite figure out how to choose a better life for themselves. That profile reflects a person whose *I am not lovable as I am* imprint is more mature than their *I am not powerful as I am* imprint. Either way, a person is still partially in the grips of the adapted identity, living in the *comfort zone* for the imprint that has not been refined.

In doing this work, I have encountered more people whose indicators of the *I am not lovable as I am* imprint are more mature than their *I am not powerful as I am* imprint. My educated guess for that difference is that these people have sought therapy, counseling, or its equivalent for their trauma. That experience allowed them to free the trapped energy underneath the bruised *I am not lovable as I am* imprint, which matured the love, anger, and release indicators to the level of Integration. However, they likely didn't have therapy, counseling, or its equivalent for maturing their *I am not powerful as I am* imprint. Therefore, the power, resistance, and individuality indicators are not as mature.

Being a magical, creative ball of energy with infinite possibilities requires you to love yourself so you can tap into your magic, exercise your power through choice, and do so in bigger and bigger ways as you partner with the field of infinite possibilities to create. This way of being occurs when all nine indicators are balanced *together*.

I want to make sure you know what this means—being open means being open to whatever arises. Emotional openings are sometimes pure joy, like an invited guest, and sometimes they are unpleasant and unwanted. In Protection, and sometimes in Expression, the emotional opening tends to be the uninvited guest. That is because our bruised emotional imprints are most robust in these states, so we can miss the subtleties and nuances of the natural emotional opening.

The EI³·⁰ Maturation Process for Indicators

There is another type of emotional opening that naturally occurs within each state. Each state has specific dynamics that, if taken advantage of, enable a more efficient and effective maturation of indicators. $EI^{3.0}$ is designed to take advantage of these naturally occurring emotional openings. Chapter 13 explains how to do that through liberating structures.

The Five Emotional States

Each person starts the emotional balance journey in a distinctive place because we have different experiences with the unwritten rule. Even though that distinctiveness exists, you will still start your emotional balance journey in one of the five emotional states. You might begin in Protection, or you may have been born into a family where the baseline maturity level was the beginning of Expression or somewhere else. How awesome.

I cover the five emotional states in the following five chapters starting with Protection. No matter where you are now, I still recommend you begin by reading the description of Protection and progress from there. To appreciate the influence of each indicator, it is best to read how indicators mature across each emotional state. By doing so, you can see connections and trends useful for your development or the development of your clients.

Each emotional state is a composite of all nine indicators at a specific level of maturity. Across the next few chapters, I explain each state in order of maturity and show how the indicators interact. Each chapter includes a summary table that specifies the maturity level of each indicator.

In the following chapters, you will also learn to identify the emotional openings that occur in each state. In The Model of Emotional Development, embracing each emotional opening creates the setting for growth and maturation.

In honor of the system-organizing principles of order and creation, each emotional state has a beginning, middle, and end. Each state is also unique, as is each state's work. Therefore, it is impossible to quantify with absolute certainty what happens in each state to each person at the beginning, middle, and end. Instead of attempting the impossible, I chose to capture the hallmarks of each state so that you can use those descriptions to self-identify. Don't worry if you're not seeing yourself more clearly right away. It is normal not to realize that you have matured through a particular state until you are fully in the next one, again validating the truth of Kierkegaard's belief that life can only be understood backwards.

If you are a big picture person, Figure 5 provides an overview of the transformational process of emotional development by emotional state as one disentangles from the adapted identity. It identifies the gift, limitation, and work of each state. The gift of each state is the benefit it offers us. The limitation of each state is what holds us back from being our best selves. Each state's work is how one takes advantage of the emotional openings that naturally occur because of the dynamics happening in a particular state. Completing each state's work matures specific indicators. That maturation process naturally develops other indicators, moving you toward emotional balance.

As I explain each state in the following five chapters, I mostly write to you as an individual, not a coach. To develop your clients to a more emotionally balanced place, you have to go there first. Thus, you are being offered the path first. Then, you can turn toward those you serve and guide them wherever they choose to go.

THE TRANSFORMATIONAL PROCESS
OF EMOTIONAL DEVELOPMENT

STATE	GIFT	LIMITATION	WORK
Protection	Safety from the many possible hurts and harms of the world	A comfort zone that masks your true nature as a magical, creative ball of energy	Dial down your anger and do something different
Expression	Empowerment	Empowering yourself at the expense of others	Create and author your life through choosing
Integration	Self-love	Conflict avoidant due to hopefulness and harmony	Refine the bruised emotional imprints
Silence & Oneness	Oneness and limitlessness	Inaction	Deepen into unconditional love and welcoming choicelessness
Presenced Wholeness	Emotional balance	Likely alone in creating, maintaining, and advancing system balance	Advocate for system balance by (1) balancing humanity and divinity in the exercise of love; (2) balancing humanity and divinity in the exercise of power; (3) embracing the infinite possibilities for your life from a place of balance

Figure 5. The Transformational Process of Emotional Development.

- There are nine indicators of emotional balance. Each one has an organic development path from imbalance to balance.

- The love indicator represents the hidden meaning; the anger indicator represents the habitual feeling; and the release indicator represents the rote action of the *I am not lovable as I am* emotional imprint.

- The power indicator represents the hidden meaning; the resistance indicator represents the habitual feeling; and the individuality indicator represents the rote action of the *I am not powerful as I am* emotional imprint.

- The energy, awareness, and language indicators work together to create the *comfort zone* and control how and when new insights about emotional development occur that allow you to mature.

- An emotional state is a collection of all nine indicators at a particular level of maturity.

- Each state has a gift and limitation.

- Each state invites us to complete specific work to take advantage of the dynamics occurring.

- All nine indicators must be in balance to achieve true nature.

- Defining moments that create the space to transform can be forced or natural.

- It is always your choice to transform.

Chapter Seven

THE STATE
OF PROTECTION

We all must start somewhere, and if you are starting in Protection, welcome. I have been here, too, and I honor the journey you will make to fulfill your destiny. Across this state a person moves through the beginning of the creation cycles for human emotional balance and emotional intelligence. Regardless of where you start, know that you found this book at this precise moment in your life because the divinity within has called your name; you responded; and now is the time. How awesome is that! Also, please know you are not alone. A sizable population of our fellow travelers is in this state, too.

Protection is a beautiful state of self-preservation where our anger and resistance are shields against the world's many possible hurts and harms. The gift of this state is that those mechanisms of self-preservation keep you safe, as they should. The limitation is that those mechanisms maintain a *comfort zone* masking your true nature as a magical, creative ball of energy entitled to a life filled with effortless joy, unlimited abundance, and good health. It is the least mature emotional state and has the most imbalanced range of the nine indicators. A person is entrenched in the adapted identity and its resulting *comfort zone*. Your rote actions are part of the deep currents that keep you enmeshed in this state. Thus, the work of this state is to accept the invitation—whether forced or natural—to dial down your anger and do something different.

People love themselves very little in this state. They are likely angry about that lack of love, and maybe unaware of their role in the situation. People also feel powerless in this state and resist anything inconsistent with their *comfort zone*. This state is known as the "To Me" state—you might feel that life happens to you and that you are at its mercy.[89] That's because the enforcers of the unwritten rule are busy telling you that who you are is not okay. The systemic influences that tell you who you get to be and what your life looks like are very loud. They eliminate any possibility of understanding that you are lovable just as you are, and the world is your oyster. In short, they are excellent at keeping you planted firmly in the *comfort zone*. Table 2 reflects the organic development path of each indicator in this state and identifies the emotional openings that can occur here.

The most important thing to remember about this state is that the blinders are not easy to remove. This difficulty occurs because the commitment to survival is strong—as it should be. If your client is in this state, initially your influence as a coach will seem to have little sway over behavior.

PROTECTION	BEGINNING	MIDDLE	END
% of Population	2%	7%	61%
Love	Absence of love	Either offering blind love or demanding it	Either offering blind love or demanding it
Anger	Blind hatred	Hatred	Focused hatred/ Focused anger
Release	*External*: Spewing violence aimed at *all of life*	*External*: Spewing violence aimed at *one's life*	*External*: Spewing hostility aimed at a specific person or thing/Spewing demands aimed at a specific person or thing
Power	Blind choosing	Blind choosing	Novice choosing
Resistance	Blind resistance	Blind resistance	Focused resistance
Individuality	Blind individuality	Blind individuality	Blind individuality
Energy	20—74 (shame, guilt, and apathy)	75—149 (grief, fear, and desire)	150—199 (anger and pride)
Awareness	Blind awareness	Blind awareness	Some awareness
Language	Life sucks	My life sucks	My life sucks/I'm great
Emotional Opening	A forced defining moment (usually violence related) or the natural defining moment of the passage of time (possibly spent incarcerated)	Same as the beginning plus an intervention or a desire to belong to a group that demands more emotionally mature behavior	Same as the beginning and the middle plus doing something different

Table 2. Development of Indicators in Protection.

Here, the level of anger and its associated action mask love, blocking us from working directly with it. We must first address this scab on the wound created by the lack of love. Doing so honors order. It means we must start with the last output and work backward, stripping the layers in reverse order. Since the release is the last output of the emotional imprint in the sequence of meaning, feeling, action, it is the place the journey starts.

Anger in this state is extreme, pervasive, and has four shades. There is blind hatred, hatred, focused hatred, and focused anger. There are four distinct ways to act upon the feeling of anger as it matures from blind hatred to focused anger:

1. Spewing vindictive and destructive violence *aimed at all of life.*
2. Spewing vindictive and destructive violence *aimed at one's life.*
3. Spewing hostility *aimed at a specific person or thing.* Hostility can lead to physical violence in some instances.
4. Spewing demands *aimed at a specific person or thing.* Demanding can lead to physical violence, but that is usually a last resort.

Thus, across the beginning and the middle of this state, the scope of the rote action narrows substantially. It represents the dialing down of the volume of anger. In the end of Protection, once the volume of anger has dropped, the blinders of the drama roles begin to impact a person.

The Beginning of Protection

To understand the depth and breadth of the patterned response at the beginning of Protection, we must first understand the force of the bruised version of the *I am not lovable as I am* emotional imprint. This bruised emotional imprint sits at the heart of emotional imbalance and doesn't easily let go of its position. Love, in other words, is complicated.

The *I Am Not Lovable as I Am* Emotional Imprint

The range of the love indicator in The Model of Emotional Development covers a lot of ground, but not at the beginning of Protection. The absence of love defines this space. Here, a person can't see, know, or feel the love.

In the beginning, a person is blind to their hatred of self and others. Instead of acknowledging and processing that hate (because they likely have no mechanism for doing so), they unknowingly project it onto all of the world, with an intensity that reflects the depth and breadth of blind hatred.

Here, anger and its release are at their most imbalanced and harmful when the bruised emotional imprint of *I am not lovable as I am* is triggered. This happens easily and regularly here. The patterned response is blind hate manifesting as a destructive force aimed at *all of life*. This type of response is all-consuming; it's pure fight or flight —no other options are available. People can easily get lost in this overwhelming hatred, unable to see any way out of their situation except physical violence. It is also doing exactly what it is supposed to do—guarding against further hurt and harm. The feeling is so fierce that the person has no awareness that their patterned response is attempting to show them something about themselves. Instead of getting that message, they see only hatred, unfairness, injustice, or just plain evil all around them.

Blind hatred is not the same as feeling angry toward someone you believe has deliberately done you wrong; it's bigger than that. From this perspective, everything feels like a slight. The world is simply miserable, evil, hopeless, or horrible. You feel betrayed by all of life. You have no tools for processing feelings that arise. Without any means to process, the only thing that seems clear is that whatever has happened to you was someone else's fault—not yours. You project your feelings onto others and blame them for your pain.

The tremendous anger of Protection has taken over when a simple foul call in a youth basketball game escalates to parents and team members assaulting the referee. It's what's behind road rage, which can be set off by something as small as a simple lane change. Road rage incidents that may not make sense to you, where people are shot for what feel like minor slights (like cutting off another vehicle on the highway or not allowing a car to merge) happen because of the depth of blind hatred that percolates inside a person at the beginning of Protection.

That level of anger gives rise to an *I am going to get you before you get me* mentality, which is an appropriate stance of Protection. When a person or experience comes along and pokes the bruised emotional imprint, you'd better look out. This mentality can cause situations to escalate to violence quickly and dramatically. It can turn the simplest of exchanges into a duel to the death.

One reason our patterned response grows so large and dangerous is that many of us don't have a technique for identifying, addressing, and processing our feelings. Since we have no safe release valve for our feelings, particularly the negative ones, they continue to build. Because the blind hatred is so intense, almost everything offends a person. This quickly leads to system overwhelm. The blinders go on. At some point, the feelings boil over. A person may find themselves in a constant state of boiling over, with hatred spewing out into their lives in destructive ways repeatedly.

For people at the beginning of Protection, the blind hatred seems destined to go on forever. In reality, there is only so much of it. The struggle to manage the depth and breadth of that hatred and its associated violence defines most of this state. I refer you to Dr. Hawkins's poignant description of this struggle previously offered in Chapter 5:

> We have become afraid of our inner feelings because they hold such a massive amount of negativity that we fear we would be overwhelmed by it if we were to take a deeper look. We have a fear of these feelings because we have no conscious mechanism by which to handle the feelings if we let them come up within ourselves.[90]

During the beginning of Protection, the spewing of violence seems like a useful release valve. Most of us are familiar with spewing. Spewing means we are dumping the pain and hurt on the outside world. In essence, we project our hurt onto the rest of the world and blame the world for what we feel.

The spewing of violence offers a momentary and false sense of satisfaction. This outward expression releases just enough of the inner pressure so that the remainder can then be suppressed. We do it because it seems less painful than looking inward to address our suffering and heartbreak.

> This is a very important point to understand, for many people in society today believe that expressing their feelings frees them from the feelings. The facts are to the contrary. The expression of a feeling, first, tends to propagate that feeling and give it greater energy. Second, the expression of the feeling merely allows the remainder to be suppressed out of awareness.[91]

After we spew, we feel momentarily relieved. Maybe now, we think, the world will sort through our feelings, interpret them, and do something about them. Help from the world doesn't happen, though, because all we've done is dump the pain and hurt of the bruised emotional imprint on the outside world. Worse, spewing outward keeps us from looking inward to address our suffering and heartbreak.

We don't behave this way because that's what we want. At the beginning of Protection, a person may not even be aware that their triggers exist, let alone know if they have been triggered or understand how they are dealing with it. It can be frustrating to encounter someone in this state because you don't know how to help them. Chances are, since a good number of us spend most of our time in Protection, you are not in a position to assist others. That's understandable, because you probably don't know how to sort through and manage your feelings. If this is you, you are not alone—a large part of the world struggles with understanding their feelings and what to do with them, too.[92]

The beginning of Protection is also home to the *not enough* story, a derivative of the bruised emotional imprints. It shows up as *I am not enough* and *there is not enough*. Author Victoria Castle called these not enough stories the *Trance of Scarcity*, which she defined as "the unexamined predisposition that lack, struggle, and separation are our defining reality."[93] If you wonder what that looks like, remember people hoarding toilet paper in the United States in the spring of 2020 as the COVID-19 pandemic worsened. Talk about a scarcity mindset! When people are locked in the trance of scarcity, they can't see that a life of abundance is a reality.

The *I Am Not Powerful as I Am* Emotional Imprint

People's actions in Protection are automatic; they don't believe they have any power to choose differently. They are blind to their power to choose. Ironically, even though they may not see their right to choose, they are still choosing: choosing to hate, choosing to spew violence, choosing to be in resistance, choosing to engage in the drama roles of Victim, Persecutor, and Rescuer. They are certain that life will choose for them, and they don't get to decide for themselves. This blind choosing should sound familiar to you by now.

The habitual feeling of the bruised emotional imprint of *I am not powerful as I am* at this early point in development is blind resistance. Blind resistance certainly can feel like a lifeline when you have no other tools for surviving the emotional swell that comes at you each day. Unfortunately, resistance comes with blinders that do not allow a person to see that it is a way to shrink from life. It's an excuse for not standing your ground, and contracting in anticipation of what is to be, or building boundaries that act as fences around personal space. You are in pure survival mode at this location. You won't know the right things to resist until Expression, when you develop skills for building boundaries and expanding personal space.

Interestingly, if you insist on maintaining your personal space with a person at the beginning of Protection, they will resist and resist hard. They perceive you as trying to limit the depth and the breadth of their victimhood, and you just aren't going to be allowed to do so.

This person cannot tease out individuality by exploring the edges of who they are. They don't understand where they end, and you begin, so they encroach on your space. If you are at the beginning of Protection, too, you do the same to them without either of you understanding how compromising that can be for both of you. This pattern of not respecting the personal space of others continues across all of Protection.

The *Comfort Zone*

At the beginning of Protection, the blinders work, which creates an almost impenetrable *comfort zone*. While I can repeatedly tell a person at the beginning of Protection that true nature is a place of effortless joy, unlimited abundance, and good health, they won't believe me. A person can see all that is happening in my life, but they are blocked from recognizing that the same can happen in their life. You will hear someone at the beginning of this state make comments like "That never happens to me" or "The good stuff always happens to other people." It is just not within people's *comfort zones* at this maturity level to know that good stuff can happen for them.

The feelings of blind hatred and blind resistance at the beginning of this state result in a low-energy signature, usually between twenty and seventy-four. This low-frequency range is reflective of shame, guilt, and apathy. According to Dr. Hawkins, the lifeviews at these low-energy signatures are miserable, evil, and hopeless. It follows then that a person with this imbalanced energy signature attracts other people and experiences reflective of shame, guilt, and apathy. Attracting others with the same low-energy signature reinforces their imbalanced belief system.

The imbalance at the beginning of this state makes it hard for a person to take responsibility for what is happening to them, and the language used reflects this lack of ownership. At the beginning of this state, you will hear people say, "Life sucks." And if all of life sucks, the thinking goes, why not band together with other desperate people to try to get ahead? The mindset of this language creates "street gangs and people who come to work with shotguns...People at this stage are despairingly hostile, and they band together to get ahead in a violent and unfair world."[94]

By repeatedly using language like "Life sucks," you can cease to think of other people as individuals. You lose sight of morality. The level of anger you are experiencing leads you to believe "there's no point to values, vision, or morality. In fact, these seem like con games designed to make us miss the obvious truth of life, which is that it isn't fair, it's a vile place, and we all die."[95] Other phrases you will hear from people in this stage include, "kill the offender," "exact revenge," or "get vengeance." Of course, there are other ways to handle anger, and they become available to us in more mature emotional states.

Maturation

So, you may be wondering, where are the emotional openings? I admit they are tough to come by in this state and very hard to use to good advantage. Disrupting homeostasis to move out of the *comfort zone* is difficult at this point in emotional development. The bruised emotional imprints are very good at guarding you. So good that the experiences the universe invents to get you to notice your actions have to be the equivalent of thunderous shouts disguised as forced defining moments. No matter the form, the purpose is always the same: getting you to notice your actions in hopes you see the habitual feelings of anger underneath them.

The person at the beginning of Protection doesn't *want* to see the openings. After all, they are rewarded for their hatred of the world—it allows them to control that world. It also allows them to abdicate responsibility for their life. If life is being "done to them," they don't have to show up and claim true nature.

This stance makes it challenging to create forward movement. It is mostly by the universe's hand that someone begins the transition from the beginning of Protection to the middle or end of this state. The emotional opening is typically forced, appearing as an unpleasant, uninvited guest. It has to be uncomfortable because it has to get their attention while they are in the blinding grasp of Protection, hidden "safely" behind such powerful blinders. Getting through to them requires a moment so forceful that it causes a state of shock in which they briefly release the armor of their bruised emotional imprints. The cognitive dissonance created must be strong enough to shatter homeostasis. That opens the way to seeing something different from the familiar ruts and grooves of the beginning of Protection. For many of us, it is the only way we will take that deeper look at our pile of unprocessed feelings, and whatever hidden meaning lies underneath.

Michael Singer calls these experiences "life-changing events." As he explains, life-changing events can be very dramatic and, by their very nature, disruptive. Your whole being is headed in one direction physically, emotionally, and mentally; and that direction has all the momentum of your past and the dreams of your future. Then suddenly, there's a major earthquake, a terrible sickness, or a chance encounter that totally sweeps you off your feet. If the event is powerful enough to change the focus of your heart and mind, the rest of your life will change in due course. You are literally not the same person on both sides of a truly life-changing event. Your interests change, your goals change, in fact, the underlying purpose of your life changes. It usually takes a very powerful event to turn your head around so far that you never look back.[96]

Author and leadership expert John Maxwell poignantly noted that:

You will never be the same person after a defining moment. Somehow you will be moved. It may be forward, or it may be backward, but make no mistake—you will be moved. Why is that? Because defining moments are not normal, and what's "normal" doesn't work in those times.[97]

No matter what you call it, these moments are the universe's poignant way of inviting us to reevaluate our lives. For people at the beginning of Protection, the defining moment may be getting arrested, being convicted of a crime, spending time in prison, surviving the violent death of a friend or family member, or some other similarly compelling and violent event. Such a moment is designed to break through all the defenses and blindness of Protection by creating a profound shock to the system and sending a person into the loss cycle.

The Loss Cycle

Before continuing with the defining moment discussion, it feels important to share information about the loss cycle and how you treat yourself during that cycle. A defining moment involves some sort of profound loss, and it is important to offer the necessary self-care to nurture yourself through the moment. Whether it is the loss of a loved one or a restructuring of your worldview, both are intense losses. While it may not feel like it right now, letting go of the way you thought the world worked is an intense loss for which we must grieve.

As I conducted research for this book, I studied the nuances of Elizabeth Kübler-Ross's grief cycle of anger, denial, bargaining, depression, and acceptance. By standing on the shoulders of her powerful and profound grief work, I came to see that we go through a similar process during any loss. A loss cycle begins anytime we lose something, or something ends. It might be a job, a memento, a dream, the life of a loved one—and that includes our furry friends or a friend who chose your ex-spouse instead of you in the divorce.

I also came to see a sixth stage in the loss cycle: Remembrance. Remembrance is the act of remembering something we lost and the void left by the absence. Remembrance changes over time; for instance, the frequency and the duration of the pain of remembrance can diminish. But the intensity? When we remember, regardless of how far away from the loss we are, the pain can be as intense as the very moment it happened. Does it ever subside? I think so. The simple truth is that the pain of remembrance lasts as long as it lasts. However long, it's important to honor it, allow it, and be kind to yourself while you are in it. We can revisit the six stages of loss at any time in our emotional development.

Multiple outcomes are possible in the wake of a defining moment. I'm afraid I can't promise that a defining moment means movement toward emotional balance. As Maxwell notes, these events can push you forward or backward. These moments of loss might paralyze you for years, driving you deeper into the woundedness of the bruised emotional imprints so that nothing changes.

However, the shock of the defining moment can cause a person to let go of their preconceived notions about life long enough to invite them to feel grief over the loss. While a person at the beginning of Protection has an energy signature between twenty and seventy-four, grief and its companion, regret, have a frequency of seventy-five. If the loss experienced is compelling enough to break through the inculcated messages of how miserable, evil, or hopeless life is, the experience can invite an increase in the energy frequency. It can rise to the level of grief, where there is regret and despondency, and life is perceived as tragic. That growth may not sound like progress, but this shift can evolve a person to the middle of Protection.

The moment can also create fear, frightening a person and causing them to withdraw from society. This shift bumps the energy signature to one hundred. Again, this growth may not sound like progress, but it can evolve a person to the middle of Protection, too.

A defining moment can also be so disappointing and shocking that the person craves something different in their life than what has been taking place, which invites an energy spike to desire at 125. Suppose a person can increase their energy signature to 125 as a new set point. In that case, this new normal invites a shift in lifeview from finding all of the world frightening, tragic, hopeless, evil, or miserable, to being disappointed in the way one's life is turning out. The release and language indicators mature at this higher energy signature, resulting in a person evolving to the middle of Protection.

Finally, if the loss experienced is forceful and shocking enough, it can invite a spike in energy to 150. This is the place of anger without the vindictiveness of hatred. If a person's *comfort zone* expands to 150, that can transform them to the end of Protection, skipping over the middle.

Regardless of the accompanying increase in frequency, the defining moment can be the emotional opening for transformation. If a person can become curious about seeking something different, that internal inquiry can harness the energy increase and pull the person to a more mature place. It can shake them out of the deep ruts and grooves of their imprints. While these moments are designed to invite us to question our existence and how we might be living our lives, they are specially designed to help us see the depth and breadth of our destructive actions.

These life moments can happen to anyone in any state, because life happens to everyone. They can show us what we have resisted about ourselves that might be trying to get our attention. First, politely; then, quite possibly, desperately.

Finally, the passage of time, possibly spent incarcerated, can be a natural emotional opening. For inexplicable reasons, one day, a person wakes up and realizes that the life of hatred and spewing violence is no longer for them. They begin to search for something different. This curiosity can power transformation to a more emotionally balanced space.

The Middle of Protection

A person enters the middle of Protection with an energy signature between 75 and 149, encompassing the levels of grief, fear, and desire. Being in the middle might not feel much like progress, but it is. The increase in an energy signature allows people to see that they don't hate all of the world. They just hate their life. Instead of blind hatred aimed in every direction, that hatred is now aimed at a person's life.

Instead of spewing violence at *all of life,* the violence is spewed at *the people and things in their life.* Sadly, that can include themselves, in the form of self-harm, such as substance abuse; self-injury, like cutting or hairpulling; or similar actions. Even though the volume of anger has been turned down slightly, it is not enough for a person to turn their attention to anything else. The focus of existence remains survival.

At the beginning of Protection, the hatred aimed at all of life left no room for love, so it was absent. Here, the love indicator matures to blind love. We now leverage love as a tool of manipulation to get what we want in life or to sacrifice ourselves in the service of others. Blind love, either offered by you or demanded by you, is the type of love most of the world recognizes. It is a self-sacrificing love informed and energized by the unwritten rule that made you think you weren't lovable as you are. This type of love invites you to repeatedly compromise your wants, needs, and desires in the service of others because you aren't worthy of having your needs met. Or, you may use blind love as a way to control, manipulate, and diminish others to make yourself feel worthy. While this maturation of love, anger, and release doesn't seem like growth, it is.

If a person enters the middle of Protection at the frequency of grief in the wake of the shock of a defining moment, they can become frozen in that spot. Grief expert David Kessler writes, "Grief is mighty. It's easy to get stuck in your pain and remain bitter, angry, or depressed. Grief grabs your heart and doesn't seem to let go."[98] Grief is powerful enough to freeze people in place for years. In that split second of overwhelming pain created by these life-altering moments, there is a crucial choice to be made: does the moment define you, or do you define it? When such moments are allowed to define us for the rest of our days, the die typically has been cast for remaining in the middle of Protection for the foreseeable future.

Not much goes this person's way because the low-energy signature of their bruised imprints is still attracting low-energy-signature people and experiences. The *I am not enough* and *there is not enough* lifeviews remain prevalent.

As a reflection of the narrowing in the target of the anger indicator, language matures. People may stop declaring that "Life sucks" and start saying, "My life sucks." This evolution in language has been described as a person's concern shifts from a generalized gripe against all of the world to a specific set of reasons about why their life isn't working.[99] People who speak this way have "seen it all before and watched it fail."[100] Life for this person is generally, but not entirely, bad. Hate speech or broad attacks on a group of people because of a shared characteristic is still common here. Blindness remains in the form of blind love, blind choosing, blind resistance, blind individuality, and blind awareness.

One particularly illustrative example of hatred with the spewing of violence aimed at one's life comes from the January 6, 2021, riot at the US Capitol in Washington, DC. On that day, a crowd of people engaged in behavior deemed *insurrection*. The blind hatred and violent actions exhibited that day indicate the middle of Protection.

The "script" for that day will sound very familiar if you've been paying attention. First, former President Trump got people to believe that their lives sucked because the presidential election was stolen from them. The "Stop the steal" chant used by Trump and his allies was intended to implant the belief that your life will suck even more now because the election has been stolen, and you will have to live with Biden as president.

If you watched any of the videos of that day, you saw that some of the rioters were violent, forceful, miserable, and even evil. You saw people searching for ways to make other people's lives suck even more than theirs would. You saw the needless destruction of property at the US Capitol, an icon of democracy. You saw some people hunting for the Vice President and the Speaker of the House to hurt them. And they weren't sorry. Even after being arrested, many of them maintained their belligerent demeanors.

Is the emotional opening any more visible in the middle of this state? The attempts by life to gain our attention increase beyond a forced, violent defining moment and the natural defining moment of time. A defining moment in the middle can include an intervention or a desire to belong to a group that demands more emotionally mature behavior. Whether forced or natural, the moment is still an invitation to do something different.

You can attempt to manufacture a defining moment with an intervention. In an intervention, others confront a person about their actions to get the person to change. This artificially created defining moment typically is in response to someone's substance-abusing behavior or ongoing acceptance of abuse. Some interventions work, but many others don't. While these events create emotional turbulence, it isn't equivalent to a forced defining moment. Part of the low long-term success rate of interventions can be attributed to the external call to transform. Because the person for whom the intervention was arranged didn't conclude on their own that their actions must mature, the message carries less force. The onus to transform generally must be *internally motivated*.

The anomaly in the middle is joining a group that has more emotionally mature behavior and demands that whoever joins behaves the same. Joining might be a way of avoiding violence at home, in school, or in the neighborhood. This opening is not always violence-related, yet it can still create emotional turbulence for a person. If a person wants to be part of a group that will not allow the violent release, the desire to belong can create internal motivation to transform. Soon enough, the person begins to emulate the more emotionally mature behavior of the group.

Again, the emotional opening, whatever it looks like, must create enough of a shock to make a person release, however briefly, the patterns of the bruised emotional imprint of *I am not lovable as I am* to see the world differently and then act on that new perspective. While acting on an insight in the wake of an emotional opening doesn't feel like curiosity, such openings invite the person to explore something different.

With time, if a person can discover and sustain the energy signature of 150 or higher, that can allow them to *see* how destructive their actions have been. They still don't see the hatred, but they see its results.

The End of Protection

The defining moment—whether forced or natural—that evolves a person to the end of Protection matures the anger and release indicators. The maturation of these two indicators creates space for something different to occur. That something different is the realization that the person doesn't hate the world or their life. They become aware that they are angry at and hate a particular person or thing. The shift in these indicators increases the energy signature to 150, maturing a person to the end of Protection.

Two things occur when a person chooses to hate a specific person or thing and focuses resistance on that person or thing. First, blind resistance matures to focused resistance. Second, hating something or someone with specificity evolves the power indicator to novice choosing.

This phase also has a person noticing external triggers that cause spewing. The person realizes they hate something or someone specific without spinning into full-on violence at their life. This lack of violence doesn't mean they stop spewing. They are likely to spew hostility about the person or thing that hurt them at anyone who listens because that person or thing has made their lives suck. They may become aware that they are spewing but continue to do so because the underlying feelings of anger haven't been processed. If you are wondering about the difference between spewing violence and spewing hostility, I point you to the January 6, 2021, riot at the US Capitol. The people who destroyed property, hurt members of the Capitol Police, and sought to harm members of the US Congress, were spewing violence. The people who were merely chanting "Stop the steal!" or yelling other such phrases, and weren't seeking to destroy property or hurt people, were spewing hostility.

The energy signature of anger at 150 has two faces. One is constructive, and the other is destructive. Both types speak the language of "My life sucks." Paul O. writes,

> the power behind destructive anger makes a bad situation worse. The power behind constructive anger is directed toward correcting or improving a bad situation. One's thinking changes from "Isn't this awful?" to "What can be done about this?"[101]

A person whose role in The Drama Triangle is Starting Gate Victim becomes frozen in the destructive anger. The life stance that there is no personal power to change anything causes the person to resist making any choice or taking any action that frees them from the Victim role. The person has reached the limits of their blind individuality and will be frozen in destructive anger until there is a forced defining moment or the natural defining moment of the passage of time.

A person can respond to constructive anger's call to action by aspiring to correct some social injustice or flaw in the system. In this case, the behavior is channeled as a powerful platform, turning the painful experience into something meaningful. The channeling of the pain in this compelling and poignant way is an outlet for the feeling of anger. It is still doing something external to address an internal feeling, though. It is also a spewing of hostility as the person will be antagonistic and bitter about this "something" in their life that needs changing. Many great social causes arise from such moments, like Mothers Against Drunk Driving, Black Lives Matter, the #MeToo movement, and laws that protect a specific population segment.

The "What can be done about this?" question of constructive anger can also appear as a burning, compelling life question that inspires a person to seek something different. Such a question propelled me forward on my journey toward emotional balance. Something internal kept calling to me by saying, "I feel like I am supposed to be doing something, but I don't know what it is." It created significant internal turbulence for me. I began exploring how to answer that question to quiet the voice within. This type of curious exploration is a gateway to the outer edges of Protection. I have heard stories from friends and colleagues of a similar question calling to them from within, mobilizing them to go out in the world to search for answers to their version of life's compelling question.

Constructive anger's call to action can also prompt a person in an abusive relationship to finally seek safety.

An interesting thing happens as a person embraces the nuances of these small shifts and focuses on improving their situation. Over time, a person begins to demand more from life than what they have been getting. Demanding more is a shift in the person's lifeview that expands the energy signature to pride at 175.

Pride reveals itself in the maturation to "I'm great" language, which resonates with an "I am better than you" attitude. If you are looking for an example of this type of language, look no further than sports. "I'm great" is rampant in the athletic world. Politicians on the campaign trail are another example of this "better than" language. The goal is always to be greater than the other person, team, or country.

As a person begins to exercise the skills required to change or improve their circumstances, self-esteem and feelings of positivity develop, fostering pride. Pride, like the anger at the energy signature of 150, has two faces. The first is authentic pride, which is positive and generates a rise in self-esteem. The other is hubristic pride, which is negative and limits emotional development.[102] Authentic pride motivates people to be curious and demand more of themselves.

What determines the type of pride a person experiences? It's about how they manage not getting exactly what they want. At this point in emotional development, a person whose primary role in The Drama Triangle is Starting Gate Persecutor becomes aware that they don't have the skills required to improve their situation. They realize they are not going to be able to get what they want. The Persecutor is scared to look in the mirror and be truthful about this powerlessness. Instead, they blame others and are in denial about their blame game. Rather than acknowledge they have reached the limits of their abilities, they become defiant, blame others, and deny, freezing themselves in hubristic pride.

Hubristic pride can create challenges:

That's the pride that really is all about arrogance and egotism and more than just, "I worked really hard and I feel good about it." It's more, "I am the greatest. I'm better than others. I deserve more than others."[103]

The Starting Gate Persecutor is frozen around the energy signature of 175 until there is a forced defining moment or the natural defining moment of the passage of time.

A person in hubristic pride uses the language of "I'm great" from a place of self-inflation. A person in authentic pride uses that same language from a place of naturally growing self-esteem and positivity. The development of these positive feelings unintentionally resonates with an "I am better than you" attitude. Either way, we move from a language that marginalizes the self to marginalizing others.

The blinders created by the denial of hubristic pride are compelling. A prime example can be found in the Republicans in the United States who denied and continue to deny that storming the Capitol, destroying Capitol property, and threatening members of Congress on January 6, 2021, amounted to an insurrection. Other examples include people who deny COVID-19 is real and think Donald Trump won the 2020 election and will reclaim the office of the US Presidency. Because of the strength of denials emanating from people in this emotionally imbalanced location, they are clearly in hubristic pride at the end of Protection. They are likely to remain stuck there as hubristic pride can be like quicksand, locking you in place and making it difficult to mature to Expression.

That said, creating an emotional opening on the path of hubristic pride is complex; a forceful defining moment is usually required. If a forceful defining moment is not sufficient to push the person out of the end of Protection, then the next emotional opening might occur naturally. It likely occurs when a person accumulates enough life history to understand that what they are doing isn't working. This understanding leads the person to be curious and seek something different. The challenge with this method of transformation is that it can take years for a person to collect enough life history to have that realization.

Many people come to this moment in midlife. What some people call a midlife crisis isn't accurate. Instead, it is the moment people have enough life history to realize the life they have been living isn't the one they wanted—it is the life the unwritten rule allowed them to have. Because most of us don't have graceful ways for disengaging from the life the unwritten rule allows us to have, we will sometimes blow up our lives as an exit strategy. I hope this book will offer ideas on a graceful way to disengage.

This moment of awareness is likely to occur in a person's fifties or sixties. It can occur in a person's forties, but that is less likely. It can also occur in a person's seventies or eighties. For my mother, that realization happened just after her eightieth birthday.

My mother passed away on August 27, 2019, at eighty. In the months leading up to her death, she was repeatedly hospitalized. During one of those hospital stays, shortly after her eightieth birthday, she called me to say she just couldn't do it anymore. She wanted something different. I recognized the moment. She asked me what to do, so I offered some ideas. Upon ending the call, I cried because I knew that my mother didn't have long to live. In my opinion, she waited too late to attempt to change her life. I am not judging her. I have seen last-minute efforts to change before without success. I am still sad about that moment, and I am grateful for it, too. My mother provided me with a beautiful example of the power of having enough life history to know something different was required of her. Without her, I am not sure this book would exist. I acknowledge and honor the influence her life had on mine.

Another example of a late bloomer is fitness buff Joan MacDonald. MacDonald was overweight and on multiple medications for her various health conditions at seventy-one.[104] She told the media, "I was sick and tired of being sick and tired."[105] She changed her diet and started lifting weights. MacDonald is now fit and healthy. She was asked why decades passed before making a change. She offered, "It took that many years to wake up."[106] Sometimes, it just takes decades to wake up.

If a person experiences authentic pride, the growing self-esteem and positivity matures two indicators. First, it softens anger, maturing those feelings from a focused hatred to focused anger. Second, as anger evolves to focused anger, so does the release of it, moving from spewing hostility aimed at a specific person or thing to spewing demands aimed at a particular person or thing.

Even though the release matures, we still don't avoid what triggers the anger. Instead, we make demands. We demand people stay away from us. We demand they stop bringing their annoying friends by our house. Demanding is a precursor to drawing lines in the sand. Because we aren't yet aware of our right to create personal space, we don't appreciate drawing lines around ourselves.

When focused, constructive anger is partnered with authentic pride, a person can use the partnership as a foundation for transforming their life and sometimes transforming all of life in the process. Isn't that a beautiful thought? This space is where a person will channel their hurt and pain into something bigger.

A natural emotional opening occurs for a person as they gain momentum due to positive self-esteem. That momentum can carry a person to Expression. A person can also mature to Expression by exploring their anger over time. At the end of Protection, a person typically mislabels their anger by claiming they are mad, making statements like, "I am so mad at everybody, and I don't know why!" When I hear statements similar to that from clients, I know that noticing has started. It's just a beginning, as they usually have no idea of the reason for their anger. Plus, there is an external search for the cause instead of an internal one.

They don't yet understand that they have misidentified the feeling, either, because my clients aren't mad. They're angry. This natural opening of noticing and naming anger, even if it's termed being mad, can be nurtured using specific tools that invite curiosity about the anger and its origin. Some of these tools are discussed in Chapter 13. This nurturing can foster empowerment, completing the cycle of Protection and evolving a person to the beginning of Expression.

In closing this chapter on Protection, it is important to reiterate that moving through this state is not easy. To transition to Expression, we must give up a lot of imbalanced power. So, be aware; it won't be comfortable. Moving from Protection to Expression is one of the most difficult, if not *the* most difficult, transitions to make. I assure you, though, it is worth making!

TOMI'S TAKEAWAYS from This Chapter

- Protection is a beautiful state of self-preservation where anger and resistance are shields against the world's many possible hurts and harms.

- The gift of this state is that those mechanisms of self-preservation keep you safe.

- The limitation is that those mechanisms maintain a *comfort zone* masking your true nature as a magical, creative ball of energy entitled to a life filled with effortless joy, unlimited abundance, and good health.

- The work of Protection is to turn down the volume on anger and to accept the invitation to do something different.

- A defining moment in the beginning and middle of Protection usually must be forced.

- If a defining moment involves a profound loss, it is essential to offer self-care to nurture yourself through the moment.

- Table 2 maps the organic development path of the nine indicators in Protection and identifies the emotional openings that can occur here.

Chapter Eight

THE STATE
OF EXPRESSION

E xpression is known as the "By Me" state. Here, you begin to realize life is created and authored by you; you make it happen.[107] Arriving here means you have crossed one of the biggest divides in all of emotional balance: the divide between the Protection space of "I have no control over my life" and the Expression space of "I get to choose what my life looks like." Across this state a person moves through the middle of the creation cycles for human emotional balance and emotional intelligence.

The gift of Expression is empowerment. The limitation is that you empower yourself at the expense of others, unintentionally for the most part. Learning how to create and author your life through choosing is the work of this state. This time is compelling in developing emotional balance as you dare to see your anger and begin exploring power. While this state is a place of exploration, the indicators remain more out of balance than in balance. Table 3 captures the organic development path of each indicator in this state and identifies the emotional openings that can occur here.

EXPRESSION	BEGINNING	MIDDLE	END
% of Population	14.5%	5%	3.5%
Love	Either offering blind love or demanding it	Either offering blind love or demanding it	Either offering blind love or demanding it
Anger	Focused anger	Empowered anger	Empowered anger
Release	*External*: Spewing demands aimed at a specific person or thing	*External*: Expressing empowerment *Internal*: Identifying as feelings	*External*: Expressing empowerment *Internal*: Identifying as feelings
Power	Empowered choosing	Empowered choosing	Empowered choosing
Resistance	Avoidance	Empowered resistance	Empowered resistance
Individuality	Blind individuality	Empowered individuality	Empowered individuality
Energy	200—249 (courage)	200—249 (courage)	250—309 (neutrality)
Awareness	Some awareness	Some awareness	Some awareness
Language	I'm great	I'm great	We're great
Emotional Opening	Awareness that you are entitled to your anger	The qualities of courage, affirmation, and empowerment permeate all aspects of life, facilitating an expanded life view to satisfaction	Release the behaviors of the drama roles

Table 3. Development of Indicators in Expression.

Movement through Expression looks different from what occurred in Protection. In Protection, a person likely has to be slammed out of behavioral ruts and grooves to have new insights. Not so much in Expression. The energy signature of 200 encourages curiosity and active searching for what is out in the world instead of waiting for life to be "done to me." That doesn't mean defining moments don't happen in this state, because they can and do occur across the arc of life. Generally, you are better equipped to handle them.

Throughout this state, the shift to a frequency of 200 allows for feelings of empowerment to develop across the indicators of anger, release, power, resistance, and individuality. Love remains blind, and awareness remains at some awareness.

Achieving the energy signature of empowerment is cause for celebration. It is likely the most critical milestone for someone who began the journey in Protection. A word of caution, though. Even though you have left the more destructive energy signatures behind in the spiral of emotional balance, the ruts and grooves of those patterned responses are always available to you. The two patterns that seem easiest to reawaken are feelings from the loss cycle and pride. Both patterns are extremely potent and easy to reclaim.

The work of Expression continues to honor order. In Protection, life invited you to notice the rote action of your anger. Here, you peel back the layers a little more to know what triggers the anger. You also begin exploring the action of the *I am not powerful as I am* imprint. You are still working with the patterns of the imprints externally.

The Beginning of Expression

With time, the self-esteem that originates from authentic pride at the end of Protection matures and deepens into empowerment and courage. Whatever emotional opening brought you to the energy signature of 200 requires you to *explore*. Regardless of the opening and whatever you are exploring, it will ultimately lead you to the external cause for your anger. While you might have *noticed* the actions of your anger and *noticed* your triggers at the end of Protection, here you explore deeper into triggers, which mature your awareness from seeing to knowing.

At the beginning of Expression, the story of *I am not enough* and *there is not enough* remains prevalent. However, as the right to choose awakens across Expression, a person moves closer to destiny, and fate lessens its grip.

Anger can still feel overwhelming here. It is experienced as an assault on the whole person, because the parameters of their individuality have not yet been fully formed by conscious boundary setting. Thus, at the beginning of this state, instead of teasing out the underlying cause of their anger, a person continues to focus their anger outward on someone else's behavior.

As a person continues exploring the external aspects of anger through triggers and actions, they become courageous enough to avoid whatever triggers the anger, instead of merely demanding the trigger go away. This action matures the resistance indicator to avoidance. It can look as simple as no longer answering the phone when the person calling is the person who triggers your anger. However, you will tell anyone who will listen that you aren't answering any phone calls from Ann, Travis, mom, dad, or whoever you are most angry at. Thus, you are still spewing demands aimed at a specific person or thing.

The shift to avoidance is made by teasing out the edges of the self via lines drawn around anger that we tell others not to cross. As personal development writer Andrea Blundell suggests, "Without anger we wouldn't set boundaries, protect ourselves from abuse, and identify then move towards our personal values."[108] At this exact moment of drawing a line around our anger, we move from novice choosing to empowered choosing, because we choose to draw a line in the sand and avoid what triggers us. We may not recognize it for what it is, because awareness is still out of balance at this level of maturity. Yet this is a crucial step toward designing the life of your dreams.

Usually, in such a scenario, we are angry at a specific person who didn't love us in the way we wanted to be loved, or they injured us somehow. Since we have no power to change what happened, we resist that person by avoiding them while continuing to spew demands such as "Stay away from me!" or "Don't do that to me!" This location is where the person whose primary role in The Drama Triangle is Starting Gate Rescuer becomes frozen. The life stance of rescue others reaches its limits because people are moving toward empowerment and solving their own problems. There are fewer and fewer people to rescue. Here, the Rescuer must finally turn inward to rescue the self. If the Rescuer can't determine how to do that, development toward emotional balance will slow down and possibly stall at this location.

Even though we are beginning to identify our feelings, we still don't know what to do with them—so we experiment. The process can feel clumsy as someone experiments with what to resist and what lines in the sand they choose to enforce. It can look awkward and unintentionally hurt feelings, partly because the language at the beginning of Expression still comes from a place of marginalization of others. Often, people will come across like a teenager who is ultrasensitive to a parent violating their space and puts a "Do Not Enter" sign on their bedroom door. It's a clear directive to the other: Stay out of my space!

If a person doesn't know how to become curious about drawing empowered lines in the sand, development toward emotional balance can stall here. However, if a person has been doing the work of transcending their drama roles and drawing empowering lines in the sand, the grip of the drama roles begins to fade. Additionally, time spent exploring anger reveals to a person that they are entitled to their anger. This realization is the shift that transforms a person into the middle of Expression.

The Middle of Expression

The middle of Expression can be a magical time of self-discovery. As a person realizes that they are entitled to their anger, they own it. The first indication of owning this anger is that they release anger by expressing their feelings accurately and may unknowingly include the reason for the offense. It sounds like this: "I am angry about what you did because you trampled on me (in some way, shape, or form)." This type of statement represents two shifts. First, it represents the identification of the self as the feeling, adding an internal element to the release indicator. Here, a person doesn't yet realize they aren't their feelings, so they use "I am" to signify that identification. Those feelings are part of you at this point in emotional development, because you are still carrying most of them around in the emotional scrapheap. However, feelings are something you experience and let go of. As a person moves toward balance, an awareness of separating yourself from your feelings will develop. Second, uttering these words or something like them signifies the beginning of ownership of what will be allowed in an individual's space. It results in empowered anger.

The action of anger is shifting, too. For the first time, anger is not only expressed externally; it is also recognized internally, even if it is mislabeled as being mad or some other feeling. We realize that this internal anger is trying to tell us something about ourselves. That insight allows us to mature from spewing our feelings to expressing our feelings. We are still outwardly releasing our feelings but without the force and volume of spewing.

As a person deepens the exploration into what triggers anger, they shift from protecting themselves by defending their pain points with lines in the sand, to actively asking this question: "What is important?" Notice I didn't say "important to me." A person in this state is still not yet sure that there is a "me." It represents an important shift from merely fighting off the world to looking inward to see what the adapted identity tells them they care about and must protect. This looking inward is not about investigating the feeling of anger. It is about seeing what to care about.

As author and psychologist Dr. Leon Seltzer explains, part of exploring anger involves recognizing that it serves an important purpose:

It's essential to realize that anger is the one emotion that warrants being seen as moralistic. It has everything to do with values: the system of ethics you're personally devoted to. In fact, if you weren't capable of making an indignant assessment that something or someone was unfair, the feeling wouldn't exist at all. And by getting irritated with what you regard as wrong or unjust, you can experience the immediate—and substantial—gratification of occupying the moral high ground (just one of many reasons that anger can be so seductive!).

For example, if you're fired from a job you believe you've performed well, and your boss can offer you no credible explanation for letting you go, you'll almost automatically experience the disgruntlement of anger. After all, your fundamental sense of fairness has been violated. And the same holds true for situations in which you feel taken advantage of or exploited. On a somewhat less personal level, if you firmly believe that the minimum wage should be raised and you learn that Congress has refused to allow this, your perception of injustice will also lead you to experience righteous anger.

So what's so positive about your annoyance or umbrage? Simply that in various circumstances when you're not getting what you want— and think you deserve (or the exact opposite)—your angry reaction represents a vital affirmation of self-worth. It's a self-confirming protest against what offends your moral standards, what feels inequitable or reprehensible to you.[109]

In other words, anger is a warning signal representing a vital affirmation of self-worth. Isn't that a beautiful reframe? Unfortunately, few of us learn this distinction, as the unrelenting hatred and anger of Protection and focused anger at the beginning of Expression can blind us to this nuance. It certainly wasn't one I was taught. Unless someone shares this concept with you or you read it somewhere, you have no idea that anger is a warning signal indicating that a value is being violated.

Part of nurturing the dynamics in the middle of Expression is understanding that anger is a warning signal. We discover what we care most deeply about by experimenting with drawing lines in the sand. This experiment is us dipping our toes in the water of personal power. It might be a while before we can swim to the other shore, though. Because we don't have a lot of experience behind us, we might make choices that take us away from our individuality, instead of toward it.

People develop an aspect of individuality by discerning what they deeply care about and defending it. While a person most likely will not refer to this as value discovery, that is what it is. Across this state, we begin to understand what we like and don't like in our space. We stop allowing all sorts of people and things in our space that may compromise who and what we are. Additionally, as the edges of a person's values and boundaries become clear across Expression, they exercise empowered individuality by refining and deepening into what they care most deeply about. A person will begin to resonate this facet of their individuality into the world. As the nuances of the unique personality are developed, the influence of the drama roles fades more.

Building boundaries around values teaches a person what to resist, so that they resist only that which offends instead of resisting everything or the wrong people and things. This behavior is empowered resistance in action.

As choosing matures, people move away from the Protection language of "I want" to the Expression language of "I choose." This choosing plants three seeds:

1. A person begins to believe *they have the right* to choose.
2. A person begins to believe *they are entitled* to be whomever they choose to be.
3. A person starts to believe *they are entitled* to a safe space all their own.

These seeds, in turn, ultimately grow into this belief: I am entitled to personal space, and I get to be whatever I choose to be. Though these seeds don't break ground until Integration, they must be planted now in preparation for that state's dynamics.

To recap, by exploring values and boundaries, and learning and appreciating that anger is a warning signal, a person engages in empowered choosing, empowered anger, empowered resistance, and empowered individuality. A lot of personal power is being developed in the middle! To continue expanding personal power, a person may explore other qualities of individuality, including strengths and purpose.

As a person approaches the outer edge of the middle of Expression, the awareness that grows alongside boundary development and the desire to avoid hurting others' feelings as boundaries are enforced create curiosity around language and how one speaks into the world. A person begins to seek the empowering exchange. Pursuing such an exchange in the middle of Expression is the birthplace of the balanced exchange that is indicative of Presenced Wholeness. The balanced exchange is the most balanced form of engaging others.

This type of exchange is a liberating structure discussed in Chapter 13. When we are not talented at the balanced exchange (and for years I was not), we can create and compound existing interference in the system.

This notion of an empowered exchange invites a person to seek the words to build boundaries that feel more empowering, which result in statements like these:

- Hey, that crosses a line for me.
- This isn't right.
- I am not interested.
- This isn't for me.
- This infringes on my personal space.

This speech is reflective of an inside-out boundary holding. It's another milestone on the journey inward.

Here, even though a person understands what triggers anger, it can still appear at inopportune times. Anger expressed at the wrong moment or in the wrong way can bite a person in their rear end across Expression and into Integration. People will be puzzled when anger sneaks up on them because they think they have learned to manage it. News flash: they haven't. All a person has done at this point is *notice* and *own* anger. They have not yet processed or refined the feelings of anger from the foundational emotional experience, which usually doesn't occur until Integration.

As time passes, if a person is pleased with knowing their values and boundaries, they can stop exploring here, at the divide between the middle and end of Expression. Here is an excellent place to be; it can afford a good life. It is also possible that, across time, the qualities of courage, affirmation, and empowerment permeate all aspects of life, facilitating an expanded lifeview of satisfaction at the energy signature of 250. This satisfaction opens the door to the end of Expression.

The End of Expression

As satisfaction seeps across a person's life, it nurtures neutrality and invites a person into the end of Expression. As a person embraces this neutrality, they let go of polarizing dichotomies like right-wrong or good-bad. As part of this letting go, a person can begin to refine values and boundaries, seeking to understand how they use their values in relationship with self and others from a place of neutrality rather than from a place of marginalization. Exploring other qualities of individuality like strengths and purpose continues to be of interest. There is an awareness that if you understand all the different aspects of yourself, you won't marginalize who you are anymore.

This neutrality seeking matures language from "I am great" to "We're great." This language reflects a wish to create neutral relationships with the people in our lives instead of marginalizing them. In this neutrality, we seek to empower ourselves and others in our lives so that the exchange minimizes no one. Ironically, inherent in the "We're great" language is they're not. While we will actively seek not to marginalize the people in our lives, we will marginalize those outside our circle, usually unintentionally.

At the end of Expression, you live your values and the boundaries built from those values. You become curious about what you selected, experimenting to see if those values and boundaries are genuinely aspects of who you are. You can try on different personality aspects to see if they suit you. That can look messy. People in this stage might appear whimsical or capricious, even inconsistent and flaky, because of the constant and sudden change in likes and dislikes. This variability merely indicates that the person is experimenting with what individuality looks like out in the world.

One of the natural benefits of developing your individuality is that you can allow others space to do the same. Instead of seeing behavior that is not aligned with your values as a threat, you become more flexible and develop an appreciation that the other person is simply honoring their values.

Other halo effects result from maturing the individuality indicator. As you begin to cordon off your personal space, you extend that same benefit to others. As you deepen into making major life decisions using your values, you become more satisfied with yourself. As you learn that conflicts with others can be rooted in a values clash and are not purposeful attempts to annoy you, you experience less conflict and tension. As your internal choices align with higher-frequency people and experiences out in the world, you experience even greater satisfaction with life and your place in it. You also become more accepting of others and yourself. We begin to allow others their PQ, IQ, and EQ just as they are. This level of honoring the mandate of belonging is powerful and invites symptoms in the system to diminish.

At the end of Expression, we realize how wonderful it is to feel empowered. We have learned to trust ourselves with our power. We have stopped seeking permission from others to be who we are, even though we generally don't realize we have withheld that permission from ourselves until Integration. As we develop trust in ourselves, we can extend that trust to others.

If you wonder what trusting yourself looks like, I have an example. People in Protection or the beginning or middle of Expression make statements such as, "You have to earn my trust." That person is saying that they don't trust you, themselves, or the universe. Once a person matures to the end of Expression, their language around trust changes. They might now say something similar to this, "I extend trust to everyone until they show me otherwise."

As we learn to trust ourselves and the world, our awareness matures. At the end of Expression, that trust has us processing the loss cycle differently. It doesn't mean we don't experience feelings associated with the loss cycle, because we do. It just means we experience the loss from a place of trusting the natural order of life.

We recognize life is fleeting, and people and stuff come, and people and stuff go. We begin to trust that everything has a season and Mother Nature knows when the season must end. In this space, we dare to face what the death of a loved one means for us and trust that all will be well, moving us through the loss cycle in a shorter time frame.

At the very end of Expression, because we have seen how to express ourselves in a new, empowering way, we fully release the behaviors of the drama roles. As we percolate across time in these new ways of being with neutrality, trust, and release, we trust ourselves to choose wisely so we don't resist when we are asked to do so. The release of the last remnants of these drama roles matures the energy signature to willingness, at 310, which moves us into Integration. Even though we have released the drama roles and any resistance to powerlessness inherent in them, we still maintain our resistance to the way life is and our foundational emotional experiences.

While there are three more states to cover, it is essential to emphasize the power of developing deep into the state of Expression. Even if you choose not to mature past the end of Expression, I promise life will still be better for you in many amazing ways. Discovering and living from your individuality is a radical act of power that many people never attempt. You place yourself in a unique class by maturing to this moment. No one will fault you for stopping at this point on the emotional balance journey. I sure won't. However, if becoming who you came here to be is a calling you can't deny (and I couldn't deny it), then read on.

TOMI'S TAKEAWAYS from This Chapter

- Maturing to the energy signature of 200 at the beginning of Expression is likely the most critical milestone for someone who began the journey in Protection.

- The gift of this state is empowerment.

- The limitation is that you empower yourself at the expense of others, unintentionally for the most part.

- Learning how to create and author your life through choosing is the work of this state.

- The powerful dynamic at play in Expression is the development of individuality.

- Table 3 maps the organic development path of the nine indicators in Expression and identifies the emotional openings that can occur here.

Chapter Nine

THE STATE
OF INTEGRATION

The belief that *life is authored by me* that dominates in Expression is replaced in Integration with the belief that *life wants to emerge through me.*[110] How do we allow what wants to emerge through us to do so? We must turn inward to accept and integrate the emotional scrapheap. As Michael Brown puts it in *The Power Process,* "Conscious integration of our imprinted emotional charge is the pathway walked by the bravest of the brave."[111] What your bravery demands of you is set forth in Table 4.

The gift of Integration is self-love. The limitation is that the hopeful and harmonious lifeviews experienced in this state can make us conflict-avoidant. The work of this state requires us to turn inward to refine and process our anger. Doing so allows the heart to open so we can experience self-love. Across this state a person moves through

INTEGRATION	BEGINNING	MIDDLE	END
% of Population	←——————— 6% ———————→		
Love	Either offering blind love or demanding it	Either offering blind love or demanding it	Self-love
Anger	Inner anger	Inner anger	Absence of anger
Release	*External*: Expressing hopefulness *Internal*: Observing	*External*: Expressing harmony *Internal*: Integration of the past	*External*: Expressing reverence *Internal*: Honoring the past
Power	Empowered choosing	Intentional choosing	Intentional choosing
Resistance	Willingness	Acceptance	Revelation
Individuality	Empowered individuality	Adapted individuality	Integrated individuality
Energy	310—349 (willingness)	350—499 (acceptance and reason)	500—539 (love)
Awareness	Awareness with some embodiment	Awareness with some embodiment	Awareness with some embodiment
Language	We're great	Life's great	Life's great
Emotional Opening	Acceptance that a pile of feelings exists	Awareness of no more anger, no more people or experiences to forgive, and no more feelings to process	Allowing love to have its way with you

Table 4. Development of Indicators in Integration.

the end of the creation cycles for human emotional balance and emotional intelligence.

Maturing to Integration is another cause for celebration (and isn't every single moment of this beautiful life cause for celebration?). Opening the heart in this state is the second most important milestone for someone who began the journey in Protection. It is, I believe, the most important milestone for someone who began the journey in Expression.

Remember, even though we have left behind the more destructive energy signatures in the spiral of emotional balance, they are always available to us. The pattern that seems to be the easiest to reawaken in this state is pride. More is offered on pride in the section on the end of Integration.

The Beginning of Integration

The willingness that occurs at the energy signature of 310 has a trickle-down effect at the beginning of Integration. First, maturation of the resistance indicator to willingness means we are no longer resisting the external world. Time spent trusting the universe at the end of Expression taught us to let go of our patterned behavior of externally pushing back on what life delivers to us. We are willing to engage the world and ourselves in new ways. Second, the optimism and hopefulness that accompany the energy signature of 310 make us hopeful about life, so our release of anger matures to expressing hopefulness. Third, willingness deepens the internal element of release. We are willing to look inward to observe what happens when our emotional imprint is triggered, rather than merely identifying with the feeling. Finally, when we look inward to observe our feelings, anger shifts as well.

We realize that we have been angry at the external world in the past. Now, rather than foisting our anger on the outside world and expecting someone else to dissect it, explain it, interpret it, or clean it up, we willingly turn inward to examine what truly angers us. This turning inward is an intentional act. We willingly and intentionally choose to look inward for the source of our anger beyond a value that is being violated (which is an external cause). Here, we observe our anger but don't attempt to engage it. This moment of observing allows us to realize that the outside world never really helped us manage our feelings and that the person we are truly angry at is ourselves. We don't spew violently about it. We are hopeful that we will understand more about managing our feelings, so we can express optimism about ourselves, others, and the world. We can be conflict-avoidant to maintain our hopefulness and optimism, moving away from tensions instead of speaking into them.

Here, the love indicator remains at blind love; the power indicator remains at empowered individuality; and the language indicator remains at "We're great." The awareness indicator remains the same as well, because we continue to see and know new information while beginning to embody some of the information we already know. For instance, we begin to embody the individuality we developed across Expression. It is unnecessary to think about living aligned with the different aspects of our individuality in Integration. We have practiced it so much, it is now ingrained in who we are. We embody that uniqueness.

Remember, embodiment is the highest form of knowing. It allows us to *feel* the truth of EI³·⁰ and its various elements, processes, and indicators. The more embodiment is embraced, the more the heart opens. Embodiment is an essential element of emotional balance; we are required to bring our heads and hearts together for balance to occur. We cannot intellectualize our way to emotional balance.

As we make this intentional turn inward to see more of the internal landscape of our anger, we discover all these unprocessed feelings lying around. Steven Covey advised that those feelings that remain unexpressed "will never die. They are buried alive and will come forth later in uglier ways."[112] Oh, how familiar I am with those uglier ways. Integration provides the space for that moment of reckoning.

As Marc Brackett writes in *Permission to Feel*, it is necessary to process our feelings through an integration method because

> when we ignore our feelings, or suppress them, they only become stronger. The really powerful emotions build up inside us, like a dark force that inevitability poisons everything we do, whether we like it or not. Hurt feelings don't vanish on their own. They don't heal themselves... they pile up like a debt that will eventually come due.[113]

In the wake of discovering all that is clanging around on the interior, we have an insight into our experience in Expression. In that state, we *saw* our triggers; we *saw* how we released anger; we came to *know* the external cause of anger; and we might have *owned* that anger; but we never *felt* it.

We now must choose. Do we rest here, willing to observe the emotional scrapheap and do nothing about it? Or do we accept the scrapheap and then process it? Choosing to rest here is not a bad thing. Integration is rarefied air. Only about 6 percent of the adult population has matured to this state. If we choose to process whatever is in the scrapheap, and it is always your choice whether you do that or not, we take advantage of the naturally occurring emotional opening. Because of the depth and breadth of the feelings in the scrapheap, it is a good idea to have someone help nurture you through this opening.

Choosing to sort through the emotional scrapheap signals an acceptance that a pile of feelings exists. It doesn't signal an acceptance of each one, but it does indicate that we see the pile, and now we are ready to do something with it. Acceptance of this pile of feelings expands the energy signature to 350 and transforms a person to the middle of Integration.

The Middle of Integration

Acceptance of that pile of unprocessed feelings generates motion and fireworks in the middle. Let's start with the motion. First, accepting the emotional scrapheap creates an awareness that we, and not the world, were always bruised. Doing so matures empowered individuality to adapted individuality. We see how we adapted our self-image regarding love to fit the needs of the unwritten rule, and we accept it. Accepting our bruises is partially attributable to the increase in the energy signature to 350, which brings a harmonious lifeview. This lifeview has us seeking harmony in all aspects of our life, first and foremost with ourselves. I define harmony as "compatibility; internal calm; good rapport; agreement among all elements." That internal calm is what we seek within ourselves. What we seek externally is compatibility and good rapport. Agreement among all elements is what we seek when we bring the external and the internal together. Seeking harmony preoccupies us at this phase and impacts how we engage the world. We seek a harmonious exchange with all of life, which evolves language to "Life's great." To maintain harmony with ourselves and others, we will actively avoid conflict.

We realize that harmony can only happen internally if we intentionally choose to accept those feelings from the past. Even though we may seek internal calm, if we have no process for refining our bruises, or we don't know how to pursue nurturing for this opening, our journey to emotional balance can stall here.

Let's look at why there are internal fireworks. The work across the middle is focused on processing the feelings in the emotional scrapheap so the heart will open. This process is filled with meaningful moments aimed at examining the made-up parts of who we are, and it is learning to intentionally choose differently for ourselves. Only when we've done that can we open the heart to embrace self-love.

That can be a challenge because many of us, me included, shut off our hearts from feeling as we grew up, which blocked off this avenue of knowing, and we became hard-hearted. In other words, we became emotionally numb. We may have felt there was no other option—staying open to feeling made us too vulnerable or overwhelmed. I imagine that is what happened for my mother at the courthouse steps as she watched her father walking away while still grieving her mother's loss. The echo of the boom as she slammed the doors on her heart still reverberates in my life.

Bestselling author and counselor Dr. Deborah MacNamara offers an explanation of the loss that results from emotional numbing, or slamming the doors on the heart:

Hearts can grow cold and become hardened—something poets, artists, and musicians have always claimed. From children to adults, emotional numbing is part of the human condition and reveals the inherent vulnerability in a system that was built to feel deeply. As Hank Williams lamented, "Why can't I free your doubtful mind and melt your cold, cold heart?" The loss to human functioning is tragic, as it is our caring that makes us fully human and most humane.

Today we have neuroscience mapping out how emotional inhibition occurs within the limbic system. At last, Freud's theory of how we can be driven by unconscious emotions has gained its neuroscientific footing. Every brain comes equipped with the capacity to tune out what distresses, repress bad memories, dull the pain, suppress alarming feelings, and be divested of caring and responsibility. The anthem of the emotionally defended is, "I don't care," "doesn't matter," "that doesn't bother me," or "whatever," and resounds loudly among our kids (and many adults) today.[114]

I add that the "caring that makes us fully human and most humane" happens in Presenced Wholeness when all of the indicators are in balance. The door to that caring opens here in Integration, when we learn how to care about ourselves first, our authentic selves, and not the adapted identity who has been in charge all along. To do that, we must intentionally choose to open our hearts and feel all the unprocessed feelings from days gone by.

Here in the middle, empowered choosing matures to intentional choosing. This transformation occurs as we intentionally choose to accept the feelings in our scrapheap, and when we intentionally choose to open our hearts.

Why is it important for the heart to open? The heart is capable of holding the intellect of the mind and the mystery of our divinity without questioning the validity of one or the other. Thus, reconnecting to the heart allows us to reclaim the divinity within. That is the doorway to Silence & Oneness.

If you are able to integrate the past and open the heart, then by the end of Integration, the bruises of your *I am not lovable as I am* imprint will no longer guard you. Author, visionary, consultant, and creative change agent Lior Arussy offers that our experiences shouldn't limit us, observing that

> the life lessons we carry with us can help us avoid mistakes and minimize pain, but they should not block our progress. We should be very conscious of those preconceived notions and open our eyes to the world of possibilities around us.[115]

A refining process allows us to expand our *comfort zone* so we can see how much bigger our love can be in this infinite universe.

Before further exploring that scrapheap of unprocessed feelings, let's talk about what acceptance looks like. I explained my understanding of acceptance to a client one day. When I was finished with the explanation, she said, "Doesn't that make me a doormat?" I chuckled and replied, "It might look like that to other people. But it doesn't. And it doesn't matter what other people think." I think Dr. O. said it wisely: "Acceptance does not mean submission to a degrading situation. It means accepting the fact of a situation, then deciding what we will do about it."[116]

Acceptance is not about submission. It is about giving permission to ourselves to receive the way something happened. Giving permission doesn't mean we like it, just that we are in acceptance of that experience. My version of acceptance is saying, "I understand and appreciate the way the moment was, and that doesn't mean I have to like it." The key to acceptance is first freeing yourself from the hurt or wrong you have embraced. When you can accept everything just as it took place, you remove the charge of the trigger. At this point, our bruised emotional imprints begin to surrender their role as guards. However, we don't become aware of how to use those imprints as guides until we mature to Presenced Wholeness.

Remember, just because you accept something doesn't mean you like what took place. You get to have your feelings about the experience.

Learning to accept these past painful feelings gives rise to the awareness that the universe is benevolent and each moment is for you, whether you like it or not. As Howard Falco writes, the universe supports your evolution and transformation:

> One of the most powerful realizations you can come to on your journey of awareness is that the universe is here to serve you. This is not some egotistical notion of specialness or separateness, but something much more empowering and profound. Life serves the continuation of life.[117]

Don't worry if this idea seems untrue to you right now. Over and over, I read and listened to people telling me the universe is benevolent and that everything is for me, so accept it instead of resisting it, but I couldn't quite wrap my head around the concept. It wasn't until I was in a Coaches Rising workshop in the fall of 2018 with the delightful Jim Dethmer that I finally understood what a benevolent universe looks like.

Dethmer, who was leading the workshop, explained the concept of "source" (his term for the field of infinite possibilities) and how to coach from that place. I wasn't really tracking his explanation until he offered an example. He told us he had been observing a videotaped coaching session to provide feedback to the coach. In the middle of the coaching session, the client's phone rang. Dethmer paid attention to how the coach responded. If you are a coach in the state of Protection or Expression, and the phone starts to ring during the coaching session, you have a variety of responses to choose from. As Dethmer put it, you might say:

"Would you mind turning off your phone, because this is a sacred experience and I'd like us to be distraction-free and, quite frankly, I'm a little bugged that your phone keeps going off."

You might also have a very healthy boundary where you say, "While we're in session, I want devices turned off." That's different.

What I'm saying is you get bugged and you're resistant. This coach didn't do that. The client started to say they were sorry and turned over the phone. The coach said, "Before you turn it over, who's calling?" The coach is going, whatever is occurring in this session is for us. Who's calling?

The client picks up the phone and goes, "It's my father." The coach, not skipping a beat, goes, "Does anything come up for you when you see that your father is calling while we're having this conversation?" The client is talking about fear and her relationship to fear. She goes, "You know, my father told me from the time I was a little girl, you can't be scared. Fear isn't welcome here." Wow…Dad decides to come to the session.

The coach, who is not resisting the vibrating or the ringing or the distraction, integrates it in because she's not resisting what is. She's not wanting to control. She integrates it in and the woman has a mini breakthrough right there.[118]

Yes. What he said.

Our attitude about our circumstances is different in the last three emotional states of Integration, Silence & Oneness, and Presenced Wholeness. Pema Chodron, author and American Tibetan Buddhist, says, "Our attitude can be that we keep getting another chance, rather than that we're just getting another bad deal."[119] A person in these more mature states learns "to accept the present moment as if we had invited it, and work with it instead of against it, making it our ally rather than our enemy."[120]

Embracing the idea that everything is for you is the first step in refining the largest part of the story written in your version of The Book of Life. Doing so sets the stage for what takes place at the end of Integration. Thus, going forward, when life happens, you don't ask, "Why me?" Instead, you wonder, "How is this moment for me?" I follow that question with this statement: "Allow me to see what needs to be seen so I can learn the lesson and continue to evolve."

Typically, what needs to be seen is a lingering facet of your bruised emotional imprint that might still be running the show. You turn inward to look around to see what might require your attention. What do you need to accept to make your internal space harmonious?

I have been here many times. One moment in particular got my attention because it smacked me hard in the wallet. That moment started on Friday, February 15, 2019, at approximately 4:00 p.m., when

I received a text from my husband, Jim. I had no idea what reading it would do to our world. Here is what he sent me:

WE MAY HAVE A BIG PROBLEM. FRAUDSTERS MAY HAVE DIVERTED THE PAYOFF TO SPECIALIZED LOAN SERVICING. I am on the phone now. OMG.

We had just sold our home of twenty-two years the previous Friday. Was he telling me that the $370,000 mortgage payoff made via a wire transfer never made it to the bank that held the mortgage? And why was he texting me in all capital letters? Jim never yells—in person, much less via text.

I met Jim in law school. We are both lawyers. This kind of thing doesn't happen to lawyers, right? Yeah, well, cue the laughter of the universe because these sorts of scams can happen to anyone. Anytime. Anywhere. Even to lawyers.

As I sat in our newly leased apartment, I pondered my options. Do I text back? Do I call Jim? I had a moment of clarity amidst all the swirling fear and anxiety. In my head, I heard my friend Luis ask this question, "Who are you going to be about it?" What a great question. Who, indeed. Since the news of the cyber fraud that changed my world, it has been one of my guiding questions.

In the moments after reading the initial text from Jim, I decided that even if we never recovered the $370,000, even if we had to pay the mortgage off using our retirement accounts, even if we never owned another home because of this situation, I was still Tomi Bryan, Tomi Llama, mom, coach, consultant, Aunt Tomi, friend, lover, business owner, etc. I would not let this perceived bad thing shift me out of the adventuresome, fun-loving space where I could pursue effortless joy, abundance, and good health. I was going to be the best possible person I could be about it. I needed to accept the moment as if I had invited it, work with it instead of against it, and make it my ally rather than my enemy because this moment was for me.

So how does someone who just sold her home of twenty-two years, and executed a purchase contract on her next dream home, decide life is awesome right after she is informed that $370,000 has been hijacked by a cyber fraudster? By being curious and asking the bigger question. By understanding that life happens and being enriched by what unfolds rather than entrenched by it.

Remember when I said in a previous chapter that the more mature states deal with the loss cycle differently? This cyber fraud incident was my chance to deal with it differently.

Instead of asking, "Why did this happen to me?" I dared to ask, "How is this for me?" and "Who am I going to be about it?" The answers were that I was not going to be afraid of what was around the corner in this game called life, and I would embrace the moment. I reminded myself that I have an amazing husband, fabulous children, and a group of wonderful friends and extended family who love me. I then made another decision: Life. Is. Awesome. If I believed that life is a grand adventure, and I did (still do!), I was going to have to live those words through whatever was barreling down the pike at us fast and hard. So, who was I going to be about the hijacked mortgage payoff? I was going to be awesome about it because life is an adventure. And I love a damn good adventure.

After I internalized that perspective, I climbed in my car and drove to my husband's office to see how I might help him process what was happening. The answers didn't come right away. In that initial conversation with my husband, and every day in the following weeks, I had to keep reminding myself of the guiding question: Who will I be about it?

First, I was going to be someone who faced the facts. Yes, the wiring instructions for our mortgage payoff had been intercepted and changed by a cyber fraudster. No, the buyer's attorney's law firm did not independently verify the wiring instructions before wiring the $370,000 payoff to the bank, which is a mandatory legal practice in North Carolina, where we live. Thus, our mortgage had not been paid off. Yet, we no longer owned the property that secured the mortgage, having deeded it to the buyers during the closing. Because our house was an older home, we had a preservation group strip the house to recycle fixtures, such as paneling and a claw-footed bathtub. The house was barely habitable now. The four buyers, who bought the house to demolish and build two new houses on the lot, didn't have a clear title. It was most certainly a life-changing event.

A few more facts: On February 14, the day before the cyber fraud was discovered, Jim and I had entered into a purchase contract for another home. We couldn't complete the purchase with the mortgage from the last house on our credit report.

It was challenging not to see the whole thing as a disaster. It looked like we would have to withdraw from the purchase contract for that dream house on the lake. We would also have to keep making the mortgage payments on our old house until the situation was resolved. And we had to pay rent on the apartment. It didn't look good. So, who was I going to be about it?

Fortunately, I'd had a role model for this moment earlier in my life. In 1997, when I was practicing law, I had a case representing a small contractor who had not been fully paid for work completed and accepted by a large contractor. At the mediation, a legal proceeding to settle the case without going to trial, my client agreed to settle for half of what his company was owed. To say I was incensed for my client is an understatement. Even though the client had agreed to settle, I was still angry.

At the closing of the mediation, my client spoke up and said, "I would like to say a prayer." What? *Okay,* I thought. *Just get it over with, so I can go back to my anger.*

My client then thanked God for allowing this matter to be resolved. He thanked God for the friendship and the camaraderie. He even wished everyone well in their businesses and in life. He was grateful for getting half of what he was owed. When he was finished, I couldn't understand what I had just witnessed. My client's actions left an indelible mark on me.

I long wondered how one gets to be that generous-hearted? It was only upon entering the emotional state of Integration that I came to understand the root of his actions. He was far more emotionally mature than I was. A lot more. Like a ton more. Like fourteen lifetimes more emotionally mature than I was then.

It wasn't easy waiting for the cyber fraud to be resolved. Some nights, long after the lights were off, I lay in bed asking the universe, "Show me what needs to be seen. I know this is for me, so let me see the power of this moment." I caught glimpses of what I thought the answer might be. Sometimes, it can take years (and if you are resistant like me, it might take decades) for us to understand how an event weaves into the larger fabric of our lives.

Several years out from that defining moment, I can look back on it to see how that cyber fraud event was absolutely for me. It certainly didn't feel that way when Jim and I decided to file a lawsuit that would allow us to stop the demolition of the house pending resolution of the cyber fraud situation. That's all we felt we could do. At the time, this type of fraud had happened to many people, and very few of them ever got their money back, so we hardly dared hope for that.

Life, however, has its ways. As it happened, the closing attorney had been caught in this same type of scam a few years before we came along. To continue conducting real estate closings after the scam, he was required to obtain a cyber fraud insurance policy. Hardly any solo practitioner law firms have these policies because they are expensive.

When I found out this wasn't the first time this type of fraud had happened at this law office, I was angry. But in the end, I could only thank goodness it had happened before. That insurance policy was the primary reason we were made whole through our lawsuit and received every penny we had lost. We were able to pay everything off—what a relief.

I have no concrete proof of why we are some of the few people who got their money back. I attribute it to not being in fear of never getting the money back. I attribute it to lying awake at night, inviting the universe to show me what needed to be seen. I wasn't in resistance. I wasn't angry about the situation (most of the time). What became clear as time went by was that the proceeds from the sale of the house represented the Tomi of old; the one who was the powerless victim; the one who didn't think she was worthy of a huge payoff. When I realized I had created a life before the money was lost, and I would create an even better life after the money was lost, I engaged my power to choose, and the universe responded accordingly.

The day after the fraud became known to us, I said to Jim, "This year is going to be our best one yet." He busted out laughing and said, "Not possible." But I kept on saying it. Anytime one of us got down about possibly not getting the money back, I would proclaim, "It doesn't matter. This is going to be our best year yet." We would laugh.

And then, one day, it was the best year ever. That year we bought a magical house on the golf course conveniently located near work and play. The house has a water fountain in the backyard. I've always wanted a water fountain in my yard. It was the year I said yes to corporate America for a great job that suited my talents. It was the year we grossed more money than ever. We finished out that year with our younger son marrying a fabulous soul. It was an amazing celebration of love and family connections. That year exceeded my expectations.

I believe that we recovered all the money the cyber fraudster took because I was willing to stand in the middle of the experience and allow it. If I had resisted, I would have given the event power over me, which would only make it last longer. I certainly did not want this event to last longer than it needed! Instead, I acknowledged that it would last as long as it needed to last. I embraced it and looked forward to seeing who I would be about it. That's what it looks like when we live as if everything is for us. Accept it all because it was designed just for you.

As part of seeking internal harmony, a person continues to explore the application of the qualities of individuality. In particular, a person explores the harmonious application of values. At the intersection of looking to harmoniously apply values and refinement of the bruises, there comes a moment when a person realizes that those deeply held values are the highest and best expression of their bruised emotional imprints. They are the personal language of the foundational emotional experiences.

We have been profoundly caring about the things we were *told* to care about. These things include what our momma wanted us to care about; what the church, temple, or synagogue wanted us to care about; what our employer wanted us to care about; even what we cared about because we didn't receive in childhood what that value represents. This discovery crushed me. At that moment, I realized all that I had been told I had to be was a farce. This awareness felt like an exceptional breakthrough moment, but it only occurred because I had reflected over time, fermenting on who and what I was. It was a natural consequence of seeing the adapted identity with fresh eyes.

A collision of awareness occurs here. First, accepting that everything that happens is for us results in embracing one of the greater processes of the universe. It frees us from a big portion of what is written in our version of The Book of Life. Second, we have embraced our unique personality, and we know how to make choices that align with the deepest and truest parts of who we are. The result is our anger and resistance are no longer guards with a compelling need to protect us. It also cracks open the heart. As I experienced this collision, my heart was feeling and cataloging everything I had never felt to integrate it so it could be of service to me. My body was recalibrating, too. I began releasing my version of life as written in Tomi's Book of Life. I also begin to appreciate and embody the greater principles of the universe in new ways.

When we near the bottom of the emotional scrapheap, we are busy forgiving others and ourselves for our human ways. An important item to know about forgiveness is it's never about the person who hurt you. It is truly about *you* and how you want to live your life. "Psychologists generally define forgiveness as a conscious, deliberate decision to release feelings of resentment or vengeance toward a person or group who has harmed you, regardless of whether they actually deserve your forgiveness."[121]

Forgiveness is a natural consequence of the harmony seeking that happens here. You let go of the hurts and grudges that have rented space in your head for so long because you know it is crucial to achieving internal calm.

As you work on forgiving all of it, you gradually gain clarity around what is interference and what is true nature. Here is where you stop mistaking your bruises for the truth of who you are. This insight raises the energy signature to 400, the place of reason.

Time spent seeing the world from reason leads to a revelation that there is no more anger, nothing to forgive, and no more feelings to process. These revelations lift the energy signature to 500, a place of self-love and the end of Integration.

The End of Integration

At the end of Integration, because the feelings of anger in the emotional scrapheap have been accepted and are no longer talking to us or for us, and we are able to spend time fermenting in self-love and silence, some earth-shattering revelations occur. At the energy signature of love at 500, we have moved from experiencing insights to having revelations. These revelations are dramatic disclosures about how we see the world, revealing how distorted our perspective has been. We don't have insights about ourselves. Instead, we experience dramatic disclosures about how life is and how we have been living in contradiction to those disclosures. This is why the end of Integration is compelling.

First, we realize that we have spent our adult life up to this very moment trying to prove our significance. All our actions have been focused on proving *I deserve to be here* and *I am significant.* When you stand frozen in place by the realization that you have been working SO hard to prove something that was true all along, you may laugh or cry. The choice is yours. Now you understand that you have always mattered, and you realize you have always been lovable. It is also the moment you realize how much hatred you've had for yourself. At this moment is when you feel the hidden meaning of the story you created around love.

You might think that arriving at the felt sense of your self-hatred would be accompanied by fireworks, bells, and whistles. It's a significant shift! At this point in the process of freeing the heart, though, because the heart has already opened, recognizing self-hatred is less of an emotionally turbulent moment and more of a "huh, would you look at that" moment as you restack your universe. Don't get me wrong. It still rocks your world, but you just finished crying a thousand tears opening the heart, so the well is rather dry at this point. It is also a processing of the hidden meaning of the bruised *I am not lovable as I am* emotional imprint at its root. This felt experience includes surrendering the hidden meaning to its rightful place in the system by no longer being blind to it or denying it. We must now experience life without this hidden meaning dictating our human choices on love.

Around this same time, there will come a moment, an hour, a day, a week (whatever it takes) of grieving for all that was, all that never was, and all that never will be. You are letting go of your belief system and understanding of how you thought the world worked. It is an incredibly moving moment I find difficult to explain in human words. My colleague Burke Miller, in his book *Sacred Trust*, beautifully identifies this paradigm shift as a movement from a stance of "Difficult emotion is to be avoided or made to go away as quickly as possible" to one of "Difficult emotion is to be honored and listened to for the information and cleansing it can bring, then let go of as its service to your emotional presence is completed."[122]

I experienced this shift one morning. Grief overcame me. The depth and the breadth of my sobs scared me. I reached out to friends by email to make sure I wasn't losing it:

Have you ever had one of those moments where a song and a thought collide, and you just lose it? You grieve for all those things you lost, for all the things you found; for the way the world is, for the way it isn't; for all the not so nice things you did, for all the wonderful things you did; for the dreams lost, for the dreams found; for the loves lost, for the loves found?

Yeah, that's where I am today.

Me and a box of tissues, sitting in the middle of the refining fire, surrounded by your love and grace as I allow these deep, deep feelings to have their way with me, sobs wracking my body...emptying my soul.

I also texted my husband at work to make sure I was still in this reality, saying, "I'm going to be fine. I don't need anything. I'm just in the middle of an absolute meltdown that I have no control over. On the floor in tears. Just love me from there." While I texted him that I was going to be fine, I wasn't really sure of the truth of that statement. The grief holding me was profound and deep. In that moment of revelation, I was honoring the last remnants of my humanity.

I had finally processed the hidden meaning of the foundational emotional experiences of the story I told myself around love. This act flung the heart's doors wide open. My heart was finally free. This is different from the heart breaking open. The heart breaking open is about processing all those feelings we never felt. The freeing of the heart is about recontextualizing the meaning of events.

Opening and freeing the heart in this way generates feelings of deep reverence for all of life and especially for the road you have traveled. Your release indicator is externally expressing reverence and internally honoring the past. You have integrated all the adapted aspects of who you are, so the individuality indicator has matured to integrated.

Here, we spend time reflecting and understanding life events in new ways. The deeper meaning of relationships with parents or other loved ones reveals itself. For instance, for years, I resisted my mother's victimhood and the manipulative techniques she used to make sure I didn't abandon her. When the deeper meaning of our entanglement was revealed, I saw the gift she was to me. Without her deeply bruised emotional imprints, I wouldn't have understood the qualities of Protection in the informed way that I do. And if I didn't understand that, this book would probably never be written. The Model of Emotional Development can't be created. $EI^{3.0}$ doesn't exist. You get the picture. It always had to be her. She was for me.

At this point in emotional development, you may see, know, and feel amazing revelations that were not accessible in the realm of thinking only. Some people have referred to these revelations as mystical abilities, psychic powers, or even witchcraft. These insights are the natural result of freeing the heart, being in integrated individuality, and embracing being part of a larger system. You leverage being a partner with the larger system to see, know, and feel information you couldn't access in previous states. You also begin to embody the greater processes of the universe. I caution you to be careful here. The more your divinity is embraced and your awareness continues to expand, the more you might begin to believe you have been tapped to be a spiritual leader of others. That thinking is a trap. You are unique, and every one of us is unique. You are not special (and I say that from my clean and clear heart). That means you honor everyone's uniqueness, not their specialness. Balanced treatment for all! Everyone has available to them the level of awareness that allows them to see the world in new ways. Just not everyone matures toward it.

As with awareness, so it is with individuality. Some people take the uniqueness of their personality to mean that they are special, oh so very special. But our individuality doesn't make us special, either. Everyone is unique, and that uniqueness is to be honored. Regardless of where you find yourself in this range of humanity, pride is always lurking. Dr. Hawkins observed, "At any level, Pride can return, accompanied by the temptation to exploit spiritual titles or control over followers."[123]

When pride shows up, the impact can be disastrous. Many religious and spiritual leaders have met their downfall by thinking they were the source of their specialness. I am not saying this so we can point fingers and mock. I am sharing this knowledge with you as a reminder of what can happen when we don't pay attention to pride and its impact on our ability to achieve profound personal and professional success.

Everyone must pay attention to this; there are no exceptions. Regardless of our level of emotional balance, our human side always has access to pride. Take me, for example. Just because I understand how emotional development works doesn't mean I'm immune to its forces. My humanity is happy to tell you I am brilliant for writing this book and creating EI$^{3.0}$. My divinity knows better; it knows I was a conduit for delivering this information to the world and it takes no pride in its manifestation or any success of the EI$^{3.0}$. My writing this book just is.

As you can see, developing emotional balance doesn't mean you are immune to the temptations of life, including pride. Pride always exists in the system as a structural conflict that can limit development or derail it.

As the energy signature rises across the end of Integration, and as the absence of anger echoes across the heart, we turn inward to see that there is an internal space filled with love for ourselves. The light of our divinity starts to shine in that space. Self-love overtakes us. We realize just how much we have hated ourselves and how lovable we are just as we are. We have finally tuned into the frequency of self-love. We release any last aspects of the *I am not enough* story because we stop resisting the hidden meaning of the love imprint. Even though we don't understand what is happening, here is also the doorway between love as we have experienced it and love as a state of being.

We can sit in the beautiful glow of our self-love until the end of our time as humans, or we can allow love to have its way with us. If we allow love to work its restorative magic on us, our divinity shines even more brightly. Time and the continued expansion of love and divinity evolve us to a place of joy. Experiencing joy raises your energy signature to 540, transforming you to the beginning of Silence & Oneness.

TOMI'S TAKEAWAYS from This Chapter

- The gift of Integration is self-love.
- The limitation is that the hopeful and harmonious lifeviews experienced in this state can make us conflict-avoidant.
- The work of this state requires us to turn inward to refine and process our anger. Doing so allows the heart to open so we can experience self-love.
- The heart is capable of holding the intellect of the mind and the mystery of our divinity without questioning the validity of one or the other.
- The energy signature of love brings with it revelations about the way the world works that lead to recontextualizing the meaning of life events.
- Pride always exists in the system as a structural conflict that can limit development or derail it.
- Table 4 maps the organic development path of the nine indicators in Integration and identifies the emotional openings that can occur here.

Chapter Ten

THE STATE OF SILENCE
& ONENESS

The emotional state of Silence & Oneness is defined by silence within and a pervasive feeling of being one with everything. It is known as the state of enlightenment, and it isn't what you think it is. I say that from the human perspective because from a divine standpoint, Silence & Oneness is everything you think it should be. Across this state, a person fully relinquishes the human self to the oneness and fully embraces the divinity of that oneness. The energy signature in this state ranges from 540 to 1,000. It is the place of *divine* balance. In this place of divine balance, the human concepts of emotional intelligence and emotional balance hold no value.

The gift of Silence & Oneness is oneness and the accompanying limitlessness. The limitation in this state results from unconditional love, which is being love as opposed to participating in a notion of love. Without any strings attached, a person sees everything as complete, perfect, or that it just is. This perspective means there is no need to fix or solve anything, and it encourages inaction. Other people don't understand this inaction; they want you to act, but you don't.

The work of Silence & Oneness is twofold. First, we grow deeper into unconditional love and inaction across this state. Second, we welcome choicelessness.

Maturing deeper into this state is about fully embodying oneness. Dr. Hawkins describes oneness as a place where "all of existence takes on a different meaning, and we become aware of the inner beingness and essence of everything, rather than just its form. Because of this change of perception, the perfection of all things stands revealed."[124] What the indicators look like in this perfection revealed are shared in Table 5.

The oneness in Silence & Oneness is about recognizing that all of life is part of the same whole. Instead of being at the expense of. Instead of being in opposition to. Instead of being marginalized or minimized by. Instead of being in resistance to. There is no division between the inner and the outer. It is a middle path sprinkled with silence, joy, tears, and laughter, instead of riddled with questions like "Why me? or "This again?"

The place that you end in other states is not where you end in Silence & Oneness. In the previous three emotional states, as Michael Roach writes in *The Diamond Cutter*, "'You' ends where it ends not because it is a natural place to end, but only because it's where you're used to you ending."[125] In fact, it's where the unwritten rule told you to end.

SILENCE & ONENESS	BEGINNING	MIDDLE	END
% of Population	←	0.5%	→
Love	Unconditional love	Unconditional love	Unconditional love
Anger	Completeness	Perfection	Is-ness
Release	*External*: Inaction *Internal*: Witnessing	*External*: Inaction *Internal*: Witnessing	*External*: Inaction *Internal*: Witnessing
Power	Choicelessness	Choicelessness	Choicelessness
Resistance	Allowing	Allowing	Allowing
Individuality	Communion (sharing of individuality)	Oneness (no individuality)	Infinite (no individuality)
Energy	540–599 (joy)	600–699 (peace)	700–1000 (enlightenment)
Awareness	Embodiment	Embodiment	Embodiment
Language	Silence, tears, and laughter	Silence, tears, and laughter	Silence, tears, and laughter
Emotional Opening	Awareness that everything is perfect as it is	Awareness that you don't just partner with the universe; you are the universe	Curiosity about how to reclaim your humanity in light of your divinity

Table 5. Development of Indicators in Silence & Oneness.

The Beginning
of Silence & Oneness

Here, a person is neither in the adapted identity nor in true nature. In this state, where everything is complete just as it is and no action on the human's part is required, there is nothing to do except be. Consequently, Silence & Oneness is a place of low activity.

The silence created in Integration follows you into the beginning of this state, creating an effortless joy that is transfiguring. It creates feelings of being complete as a human. This joy signifies the beginning of Silence & Oneness. This completeness allows one to let go of the human self, maturing into communion with all of life from integrated individuality. Communion reflects a sharing in the individuality of each other. This communion invites a person deeper into the divinity that is each of us. This experience of divinity expands across Silence & Oneness.

Time spent allowing self-love to have its way with you evolves love into a more spiritual experience. As Dr. Hawkins describes, love becomes "progressively spiritualized, it emerges as an alignment with Divinity, which is the ultimate source and province of Love."[126] Thus, as a person enters the beginning of Silence & Oneness, transfiguring joy paired with increased divinity matures the love indicator to unconditional love.

Harold Becker, founder of The Love Foundation, defines unconditional love this way:

> Unconditional love is an unlimited way of being. We are without any limit to our thoughts and feelings in life and can create any reality we choose to focus our attention upon. There are infinite imaginative possibilities when we allow the freedom to go beyond our perceived limits. If we can dream it, we can build it. Life, through unconditional love, is a wondrous adventure that excites the very core of our being and lights our path with delight.[127]

Unconditional love is love freely offered to yourself and others with no strings attached. Dr. Hawkins described this love as "miraculous, inclusive, nonselective, transformative, unlimited, effortless, radiant, devotional, saintly, diffuse, merciful, and selfless."[128] As you allow this unconditional love to overtake you, there is no questioning "Am I worthy of love?" or "Are other people worthy of love?" You simply are love. Since you recognize the divinity within you and others, love is easy to extend.

Interestingly, everything we worked so hard to claim about ourselves is allowed without action in Silence & Oneness. We rest in the embodiment of everything being complete as it is, witness the completeness, and resist nothing because everything is divinely complete just as it is. We allow completeness by being a witness to it.

Once the anger indicator matures to feelings of completeness, the release indicator's external action follows, evolving to inaction while its internal action is witnessing the completeness of the world.

The witnessing happens as you acknowledge and observe the mind's chatter and let it pass without acting upon it. The "I" that is me doesn't need to pass judgment on anything or tell anyone that they are wrong or that they are doing anything wrong, because everything is complete as it is. You are a witness to the conversation of others, feeling no need to participate, allowing the quality of your experiences to be, without the need to label events or people as anything in particular. Without any interference to drive your inner dialogue, there almost isn't any inner dialogue, which drastically reduces the need to engage in conversation with others. We are transfigured here. Words tend to be insufficient to convey what we experience. Because the experience exceeds the capacity of human language, the means of communicating is mostly through silence, tears, and laughter.

At this level, Dr. Hawkins says, "everything happens effortlessly, by synchronicity, and the world and everything in it is seen to be an expression of love and divinity. Individual will merges into divine will."[129] Since everything happens effortlessly, there is no need to choose, making Silence & Oneness a state of choiceless awareness where you mostly abandon choosing. Everything is available to you, since you share in the field of infinite possibilities at every moment. You are aware of everything, yet you have to choose nothing—because the universe delivers what you need even before you know you need it. The universe will provide what is required. You simply witness its arrival—whatever it is.

Here, no one else's emotional imprints can move you from the fact that life is complete as it is. You are merely a witness to the patterns of the bruised emotional imprints of others. In this state, everyone and everything is sacred. The way you live "may or may not show a change to the external observer. However, habits and behavior, although they may appear to be the same, are no longer compulsive or driven. They can often be dropped, altered, or changed without undue discomfort."[130] I experienced this change.

For years I read every personal development, self-help, new age, leadership, and business book I could get my hands on. I attended workshop after workshop. Suddenly, I woke up one day and didn't care if I read another book or went to another workshop. The drive to do those activities evaporated almost overnight. While I was slightly puzzled by this shift, it didn't cause me discomfort. In hindsight, I understand that the interference driven by the bruises of "don't be stupid because it isn't safe" had been processed and refined and were no longer compelling and commanding me to make sure I wasn't stupid.

Here, there is a deep, embodied knowing. A person knows and embodies but generally doesn't act. Regular, everyday, ordinary pursuits are not as entertaining or as interesting as they once were; thus, a person in this state may choose to withdraw from society.

Time, coupled with expanding and contracting with the natural rhythm of life in a place of unconditional love, brings with it the insight that everything is perfect as it is. This perfection revealed indicates the move to the middle of Silence & Oneness.

The Middle of Silence & Oneness

A person enters the middle of Silence & Oneness at the energy signature of 600, a place of perfection, peace, and bliss. Bliss occurs when the soul is perfectly happy. This happiness is different from the human kind. When the soul is perfectly happy, the doing required to prove significance and justify our right to be here as a human is unnecessary. There is even less physical activity for a person; just the experience of being one with everything.

In our oneness, we surrender our individuality. Here, you have no boundaries because you know "I am everything, and everything is me." Being one with everything is different from being in communion. In communion, there is a shared individuality. In the oneness, you are all things. Because all things are perfect, you have no attachment to how life unfolds. You rest in the perfection of it all.

As we accept the perfection of all things and bask in that across time, we become aware that not only are we one with the universe, we are the universe. In this moment of awareness, we feel the vastness of who we are, accepting that we are infinite. As poet Walt Whitman wrote, "I am large, I contain multitudes."[131] Yes, you are, and, yes, you do. We also recognize at this moment how small our choices have been throughout our lives.

In recognizing that we are the universe, we no longer need to bring consciousness and intention together to collapse the wave function to create something. Here, we are the wave function.

Merging with the universe matures the energy signature to 700, a place of enlightenment, and opens the door to the end of this state.

The End of Silence & Oneness

As you deepen your embrace with the universe across time, your energy signature approaches 1,000. Here, everything just is, in the nothingness of everything that is. Activity levels continue to drop, although there isn't much more human activity to be relinquished at this point. A person spends the day just being, basking in the beauty of the vastness and of being infinite. Don't be fooled into thinking that "just being" is a small thing. You are in a place of pure consciousness. It's a big deal—the divine emotional presence in this state changes the energy signature of the *whole planet*.

This place sounds, well, divine, doesn't it? But I have to admit that sitting in pure consciousness, knowing that I am a divine being, created some challenges. I understood that if the person who matures to the emotional state of Silence & Oneness knows everything just is, and there is nothing for them to do to change the moment, they need only be a witness to the is-ness of the moment. But this position, in my humble opinion, does not serve the evolution of the greater good. At least it didn't for me. That may not be true for you.

The understanding that everything just is, and no action is needed to change anything, is perceived differently by humans in less mature emotional states. My understanding crystallized because of conversations with my two sons, Shep and Warren, about the Black Lives Matter movement. When I offered my point of view, coming from a place of everything just is, and there is nothing for me to do to change the moment, I was accused of engaging in white privilege and perpetuating systemic racism.

My comments had nothing to do with white privilege and everything to do with seeing the situation from a higher level of consciousness. Since my children are younger than I am, don't have the same level of life experience, and are not at the same level of emotional balance, I invited them to have this same conversation with me in ten years before judging if I was engaging in white privilege. My response didn't sit well with them. The claims of white privilege and perpetuating systemic racism grew louder in the background.

My statements to Shep and Warren weren't offered from a place of ego or pride, or at least I hope they weren't. They were offered from a place of unconditional love and realization that my children and I are not at the same place on the emotional balance journey. I was not judging them, either; I was just reflecting my system observations to them. And that is why I decided Silence & Oneness wasn't for me in this lifetime.

From a human perspective, Silence & Oneness is not a place of balance. You can realize we are still living in a human world if you are like I am. Other humans don't always appreciate or understand Silence & Oneness. The divine balance of this state doesn't make sense to humans.

I choose to use all my potential to make the world a better place for me, my children, their children, and others. That means fully embracing the uniqueness of my individuality and all that entails. The invitation to do that for the greater good happens in Presenced Wholeness unless, of course, your purpose is to remain in Silence & Oneness and walk your unique path from there. Presenced Wholeness is where I believe I can use my individuality to have the largest impact on the greater good and my enjoyment. You have to decide what is best for you and your emotional balance journey, as Silence & Oneness might be the perfect place for you. A person can stay in Silence & Oneness for the remainder of their human days. If your purpose is to impact the greater good from this place, then rest well here, my friend.

If you are like I am, you want to re-embrace your humanity, but how? If we choose to do so, we can reenter the world from Presenced Wholeness, where our divinity informs our humanity, and the witness can help us navigate between the two worlds. We move out of Silence & Oneness and into Presenced Wholeness by being curious about how humanity is used in partnership with divinity to make the world a better place. The more we explore this curiosity, the more we transition into the beginning of Presenced Wholeness.

- Silence & Oneness is the place of divine balance.
- The gift of this state is oneness and the accompanying limitlessness.
- The limitation in this state is inaction, which humans don't understand.
- The work of Silence & Oneness is to deepen into unconditional love and welcome choicelessness.
- From a human perspective, Silence & Oneness is not a place of balance.
- Table 5 maps the organic development path of the nine indicators in Silence & Oneness and identifies the emotional openings that can occur here.

Chapter Eleven

THE STATE
OF PRESENCED
WHOLENESS

Across Presenced Wholeness, we come to see, know, and embody emotional balance and begin advocating for system balance. Our destiny is fulfilled in this state as we "unlock the fullest and most satisfying expression of our being…we're empowered to play the hand we were dealt by Fate with integrity, grace, humility, compassion, courage, honor, wit, spontaneity, genius, and reverence."[132] I choose to be all in on that!

Fate's influence still exists here, as it does in every state. No matter how much we embrace our destiny, the immutable characteristics of fate, such as gender, race, family of origin, etc., are always present. In this state, fate "primarily serves as the vessel and structure through which our Destiny is fulfilled and contained."[133] Our humanity and divinity come together in this state, creating a sacred space where we can embrace and own being a magical, creative ball of energy with infinite possibilities. Here, the concept of emotional intelligence is abandoned in the pursuit of emotional balance of the human and the divine within. Ideally, that balance is best measured through indicators of emotional balance and not by outputs of emotional intelligence.

The gift of Presenced Wholeness is emotional balance, where the use of love and power doesn't create new symptoms in the system. Less than half of 1 percent of the world's population is in this emotional state. Thus, the limitation is that you are likely creating, maintaining, and advancing system balance alone. The work of being an advocate for system balance invites you to:

1. Balance humanity and divinity in the exercise of love.
2. Balance humanity and divinity in the exercise of power.
3. Embrace the infinite possibilities for your life from a place of balance.

By the end of this state, as you presence your wholeness, you can touch infinity and create from that place repeatedly, as you allow what is here and offer what is needed. When you exhibit your magic in this way, life's response is just as magical. What developing your magic looks like is outlined in Table 6.

PRESENCED WHOLENESS	BEGINNING	MIDDLE	END
% of Population	◄————— 0.5% —————►		
Love	Unconditional love with some imbalanced love mixed in	Whole love	Whole love
Anger	Is-ness with some imbalanced anger mixed in	Righteous anger in honor of system balance	Righteous anger in honor of system balance
Release	*External*: Expression of balance with some imbalanced expression mixed in *Internal*: Occasional integration of the recent past	*External*: Expression of balance *Internal*: Integration of the present	*External*: Expression of balance *Internal*: Integration of the present
Power	Choicelessness with some imbalanced choosing mixed in	Choicelessness with some imbalanced choosing mixed in	Balanced choosing
Resistance	Allowing with some imbalanced allowing mixed in	Allowing and offering	Allowing and offering
Individuality	Infinite with some imbalanced individuality mixed in	Presenced individuality	Presenced individuality
Energy	*Humanity*: ~500 (love) *Divinity*: 600–1000 (joy, peace, enlightenment)	*Humanity*: ~500 (love) *Divinity*: 600–1000 (joy, peace, enlightenment)	*Humanity*: ~500 (love) *Divinity*: 600–1000 (joy, peace, enlightenment)
Awareness	Embodiment	Embodiment	Embodiment
Language	Silence, tears, and laughter with a mix of love, honor & respect	Love, honor & respect	Love, honor & respect
Emotional Opening	Curiosity about creating from a place of whole love	Curiosity about how big your choices can be from a place of balance	Being a magical, creative ball of energy in new ways until your human suit expires

Table 6. Development of Indicators in Presenced Wholeness.

You are probably curious about why there is a state after Silence & Oneness, if all it will be used for is to step back into our humanity. We could remain in Integration and be in our humanity. However, that is not where we can create the most joy for ourselves and the most good for the world, while fulfilling our destiny. Only by traveling through Silence & Oneness can we appreciate and comprehend how to be the best version of a divine being having a human experience. This understanding is required for balance.

The challenge presented by the unconditional love experienced in Silence & Oneness is that we bliss out on how perfect everything is in our absolute place of peace. We feel the need to do nothing but emanate and radiate our unconditional love light across the planet as a witness to what is. That's beautiful, but unfortunately, our light may be lost on loved ones, friends, and colleagues who don't understand that approach. If you told a Holocaust survivor that the Holocaust was perfect just as it was, you would be accused of being a white supremacist. If you told George Floyd's mother that his death was perfect just as it was, you would be accused of being a racist. If I said that the riot on the US Capitol on January 6, 2021, was perfect just as it was, I would be accused of being an insurrectionist. Our human companions want us to show up, participate, and take action. As I mentioned in the section on Silence & Oneness, I realized that the unconditional love, witnessing, and being of Silence & Oneness is not a place of balance *for humans*.

The rest of this chapter focuses on finding that balance. It is easy to mistakenly think life is smooth sailing from here. It's not. There is turbulence ahead, but don't worry. You've got this for yourself and your clients.

The Beginning of Presenced Wholeness

In the beginning, a person ponders, "How do I reclaim my humanity in light of my divinity?" Having matured through Silence & Oneness to reach this moment, they have a vastly different perspective on being human. They have developed from imbalance as a human to imbalance as a divine being in a human body. Here, we must re-experience humanity in light of divinity.

The witness developed in Silence & Oneness emerges here as a navigator, acting as a bridge between the human self and the divine self. Now, there is both a being and a doing, and we can't leave either behind. If we choose to have a deeper impact on humanity, we must re-embrace the humanness we attempted to leave behind on the path to discovering our divinity. This is when the turbulence starts, as it takes time to understand and embrace the navigator's role and significance.

As with the messiness of Expression as a person experiences and embraces empowerment, a similar thing happens at the beginning of Presenced Wholeness. We have to work out how to integrate our humanity with our divinity, which can have us all over the place. It can have us expressing anger and acting upon it in a mix of balanced and imbalanced ways. That variability in how we show up can indicate a person reclaiming their humanity in light of their divinity.

I revisited anger easily as I attempted to reclaim my humanity. One day, I was purchasing a bike in a store and being helped by two salespeople and my husband. I became overwhelmed by all three people giving me instructions about the bike at the same time. I barked harshly at all of them. I immediately righted my feelings, but

I didn't understand them. I thought to myself, "What the heck was that about?" because I hadn't experienced feelings like that in a while.

While I know this now, I didn't think it at that moment: the navigator could help me. I didn't yet know how to use the witness I brought over from Silence & Oneness as the navigator, but I would soon learn.

Reflecting upon the bike store incident made me realize that reclaiming humanity is tricky. I also realized that I had created interference with the salespeople and my husband, mainly because I couldn't allow the moment to be as it was. That incomplete creation cycle required completion to restore balance.

Because I didn't realize that I had created trapped energy for myself and others until after the fact, I used a refinement process—the same one I used when I was in Integration—to free that interference. What became evident was that this was still an integration of past energy. Not from thirty years ago, though; from three days ago or three hours ago. Processing this anger revealed that it still operated as a warning signal.

As anger is re-engaged in Presenced Wholeness, there is a learning curve about what it represents. Here, anger is a warning signal about external conditions of system balance, not internal conditions. It is important to recognize anger as an external message from the system that something is out of balance, instead of personalizing it. It is righteous anger in honor of system balance.

Sometimes in Presenced Wholeness, you must offer anger if that is what system balance demands from you at the moment. This type of anger is not used to hurt anyone or be vindictive. It is positive anger. According to Dr. Mario Martinez, a clinical neuropsychologist, a short expression of righteous anger can decrease blood pressure and boost the immune system.[134]

Even though I didn't know it, I experienced righteous anger in honor of system balance at that moment in the bike store. I didn't need two salespeople and my husband to help me purchase a bike. That was system overload, not system balance.

You can see another example of righteous anger come to life through a fictional character, coach Ted Lasso, in certain episodes of the show *Ted Lasso*. My favorite Ted example is Season 1, Episode 6, where he engages in a short burst of righteous anger directed at Jamie Tartt, the team's star player. More detail is provided on this example later in this chapter.

One morning during my devoted personal time, as I continued to reflect on being both human and divine, and the relationship of them to anger, I felt this wisdom: "There are human things. There are divine things. And then there are godly things. Leave the godly things to the gods, and you do the rest." That felt profound and paradigm-shattering. Do the human things and the divine things and leave the rest to the gods. This way of seeing the world offered me several insights.

First, I realized that love had transformed again. Love isn't unconditional in this place of seeking balance, where anger is acceptable. System balance requires us to honor it by being an advocate for it. That means expressing righteous anger occasionally, as the imbalance occurs or right after it. When we interject the human element into unconditional love, it becomes a whole love. A whole love is one where the navigator emerges to show us how to honor the unconditional love of divinity and the self-love of humanity in furtherance of system balance.

This understanding about love led to the second realization. The navigator knows how to witness what is happening and can guide me from a place of balance. The navigator allows me to see both my humanity and my divinity. It looks like this in my head: "The human Tomi gets to be disappointed by her son's actions, and the divine Tomi is going to love him no matter what. Knowing that, do I act from my humanity or my divinity in this moment?" There are times to do the human thing. There are times to do the divine thing. Allow the navigator to guide you on which one to do.

When family members, friends, and clients share with me that they are feeling stuck, I ask, "Are you doing the human thing or the divine thing? Because whichever one you are doing, you might want to try doing the other one." The shared results of trying the other one (which is usually the divine thing) have remarkable outcomes.

A beautiful thing happens here with the navigator. Even though we might be in the middle of righteous anger, the navigator will filter our language through the unconditional love of our divinity. This balancing act has us speaking a language of love, honor, and respect that reflects a reverence for all of life.

The third realization involved my energy signature. To be whole love, I must pay attention to my energy signature. Doing so enables me to navigate between the frequency of being human and the frequency of being divine. From my perspective, the most effective human energy signature is 500, the place of love. As I learned in family dynamics training, the movement toward love is the liberating structure; it frees the person from whatever is entangling them. Remember, in this human space, love has incredible restorative powers:

Love is the solution for all constricted and stagnant subtle energy and can instantly unlock all negative feelings and make energy free-flowing.

Love heals all wounds, and quickly, when it is allowed to work. It is the most powerful energy in all of vibrational healing.[135]

While 500 is a high-energy signature, it is a frequency that a human embracing their divinity can operate from and other humans can comprehend. Everyone can feel the love in this space even if they can't understand it. As we move into higher-energy signatures, the closer we get to peace at 600, the more we drop into bliss and inaction.

You might be wondering how the love at 500 in Presenced Wholeness is different from the love at 500 in Integration. They have the same energy signature, yet the experiences are different. The love in Integration is self-love. We haven't yet learned how to extend that complete and total love of self to others. That experience happens in Silence & Oneness as the unconditional love of everything. Here, the self-love of our humanity and the unconditional love of our divinity come together as a love of all things from a place of balance. When balance is disrupted, our anger is a warning signal. The navigator knows how to negotiate from whole love, which is a balancing act of self-love and unconditional love.

The fourth realization included a requirement for me to allow life to happen in a new way. Since I was re-embracing humanity, I was stepping back into all the human systems, where I could inadvertently or overtly dishonor balance, belonging, or order, and not catch it in the moment. I might leave a creation cycle incomplete if I don't feel my feelings through to the end, such as when I start a new relationship and it doesn't work for whatever reason, or when a job or project abruptly ends without completion. And sometimes, I can know that what I am about to do is not the balanced thing to do, and do it anyway, creating a negative wake for myself or others.

The point in this state isn't to avoid creating interference; even if you fully embrace your balanced humanity, that will happen. It just does. The point is to refine and integrate when you notice the interference.

The Middle of Presenced Wholeness

I was aware of my shift into the middle only after the fact. I realized that curiosity about responding to others from whole love was inviting me to create from that space, too. I didn't recognize the opening in the moment because there was emotional turbulence, and it all seemed to run together. The same thing might happen to you. Thus, I share with you what that turbulence looked like so you can recognize it for yourself.

The vastness experienced in the oneness of Silence & Oneness is brought into Presenced Wholeness. It leaves a unique mark on a person. It allows them to understand that their energy, love, and power don't just run from the tips of the toes to the top of the head. These aspects of who you are travel endlessly in all directions with infinite possibilities. This place of infinite possibilities is where the creative forces of the universe reside. It makes you realize all over again how small your choices in Protection, Expression, and Integration have been. It is a felt sense of the smallness of your choices.

This felt sense is also a processing of the hidden meaning of the bruised *I am not powerful as I am* emotional imprint at its root. It includes surrendering the hidden meaning to its rightful place in the system by no longer being blind to it or denying it. We must now experience life without this hidden meaning limiting the size of our choices. While we experience this recontextualization in Silence & Oneness, it has no meaning to our humanity because we are fully in divinity. It just is. However, as we reawaken our humanity, this recontextualization profoundly impacts the human practice of choosing.

We bring the experience of infinite possibilities into Presenced Wholeness. As our humanity reignites, we proclaim, "I can call into my life whatever I choose, whenever I choose to, from that field of infinite possibilities!" At least I did, anyway. Remember, over in Silence & Oneness, "everything happens effortlessly, by synchronicity, and the world and everything in it are seen to be an expression of love and divinity."[136] Since everything happens effortlessly in that state, there is no need to choose. We misapply that concept from the human perspective in the middle of Presenced Wholeness. Thinking we can create whatever we want whenever we choose invites a person to get wrapped up in creating. Speaking from experience, a person can focus on creating crazy things that may not align with their journey of balance or their individuality. It is probably safe to say that pride takes over briefly. That happened to me in the middle of this state.

I was determined to create whatever I chose to create, in the way I chose for it to show up. I was large and in charge. My "smarty pants, test the limits of everything, watch this, bitches, and here, hold my biscuit while I do it" persona brought itself to my little creation party. Guess what I decided to bring into my life from the field of infinite possibilities? One of the most human things you can imagine: the winning lottery ticket. And not just any ticket. It had to be a jackpot of $200 million or more because that would be a BIG creation! That's right. I was going to win the lottery, and no one would stop me because I knew exactly how to leverage the mandates of creation to make that happen.

Surprise! What I tried to create didn't show up. I tried repeatedly without success. I ultimately became frustrated because I was sure I was doing it right, and nothing was happening. Then I became curious about why my creations would not manifest on the earthly plane, because I knew they existed in that field of infinite possibilities. I still hear the universe laughing about that one. And, if you mature to this location, you are likely to do this as well. It is a natural opening that teaches you about creation from the space of infinite possibilities as a *human*.

As I sat in my repeated failures, I did what I knew. I asked the universe to show me what needed to be seen. I laughed at the reply because it made so much sense. What I was trying to create wasn't part of my journey to emotional balance. What I was attempting to create didn't align with my individuality and what I was uniquely capable of doing. The insight was that winning the lottery wasn't the place that only I could fill. Winning the lottery wasn't something only I could do. I was attempting to create something that would thwart the development of balance for me. It wasn't my task to do.

The highest and best use of our individuality in Presenced Wholeness is when we cultivate equanimity.

Equanimity is an invaluable inner resource that is cultivated through awareness. It is the experience of knowing the movement of the mind without reactiveness, an experience of grounded presence amidst extremes. When the mind is steady and responsive, we can say to ourselves, "This moment is like this, and it doesn't have to be different right now. I can allow what is here and offer what is needed."[137]

I can allow what is here and offer what is needed. What a masterful description of operating from true nature.

The allowing part was revealed at the beginning of this state by having the navigator help me negotiate the moment. But to offer what is needed? What did that look like? It's quite simple. It happens when we partner with the universe by learning from the future as it emerges from a place of balance. We spent our time in Integration learning from the past and our time in Silence & Oneness witnessing others repeating history and allowing life to emerge without action. In Presenced Wholeness, we spend our time meeting the future. We see the future in certain moments and act upon what we are being invited to create as the moment emerges.

Let me offer a description of what meeting the future looks like. In the moment of allowing while being in whole love, my divinity touches the field of infinite possibilities to learn from the future. The navigator leads the way, advising me on what I can offer. Sometimes my action is to be divine by witnessing the moment. Sometimes it is to be divine by offering unconditional love. Sometimes my action is to be human by using my unique individuality in only the way I can. The field of infinite possibilities, where all things are, guides my actions, showing me what I need to offer at the moment. "You simply look to see what is being asked of you by the situation unfolding in front of you."[138] My offering is from a place of presenced individuality because at that moment, I am being present in the way only I can from the place only I can. When you are able to allow in this way, you become surrounded by a life that is built for you, not by you.[139]

We don't remain in this place of touching infinity. Typically, you will move into and out of it. It is hard to sustain our humanity in that place, so the navigator does it for us through our divinity. As you touch infinity in partnership with the universe, you will create beautiful and profound things aligned with your individuality. What happens at that moment defies description. It truly is magical. It is the moment we allow our emotional imprints to be guides and not guards.

With love and power matured fully, we participate with the navigator to look for a balanced choice that honors the system dynamics of balance, order, and belonging as much as possible and makes room for personal joy. Personal joy is important. The balanced choice should never require you to feel like you are sacrificing personal needs for the greater good. Sacrificing your needs is not necessarily balanced. Sometimes the balanced choice requires patiently waiting for the navigator to signal that it is time to act so neither your humanity nor divinity is marginalized. Dare I say that it, too, is a balancing act?

With the help of the navigator, we integrate imbalance in each moment. Ideally, in this state, because we are fully present for the moment in front of us, and because the bruises of our imprints have been refined and are no longer guarding us, we recognize the warning signal from the system. We immediately process the experience and any related feelings through the navigator, who points out the divine meaning and the human feelings, allowing any imbalance to rest at the moment of creation. Thus, in the present moment, there is a resting of the interference to the moment, not a releasing of it to a past moment. You want to be a clear energy channel for effortless joy, unlimited abundance, and good health. You do that by integrating interference in each moment using the navigator.

Even though you are emotionally balanced in this state, you can still encounter resistance. If you do, it is likely from the system and not you. If you are feeling blocked, out of balance, or angry in this state, I recommend working with those items at the system level instead of at the individual level to see what might be out of balance.

Because all nine indicators are in balance, true nature is embodied. A person is operating with personal congruence. That person shows up in the world authentically expressing their individuality, and others sense it, too. What does that look like? I am picturing a few real people—His Holiness the 14th Dalai Lama, Barack Obama, and Jimmy Carter—and one fictional character—Ted Lasso. There are more role models, but an extensive list is not needed to make my point.

How did the three *actual* people make my list of role models for Presenced Wholeness? The Dalai Lama was an easy choice. The principal commitments of the Dalai Lama are first to the happiness of humanity and second to harmony among the world's religions.[140] These commitments sound like a balance of humanity and divinity to me.

Barack Obama and Jimmy Carter created organizations that seek balance globally. Upon completing his second term as US President, Barack Obama created The Obama Foundation. Its mission is to inspire, empower, and connect people to change their world. That work includes the Community Leadership Corps that brings together rising leaders to identify and address community issues. It includes My Brother's Keeper Alliance that focuses on mobilizing mentors, reducing youth violence, and improving life outcomes for boys and young men of color. It includes the Girls Opportunity Alliance that empowers adolescent girls worldwide through education. The work of the Foundation seeks to create, maintain, and advance balance in an imbalanced world.[141]

After serving as US President, Jimmy Carter founded The Carter Center. Its mission is "Waging Peace. Fighting Disease. Building Hope." The goal of The Carter Center Human Rights Program is "a world where all people have the freedom to enjoy equally all their human rights so as to reach their full potential and live in dignity." The goal of the Carter Center Conflict Resolution Program is to "prevent, mitigate, and resolve conflicts to build transformative and sustainable peace." They serve all over the globe. His Center seeks to create, maintain, and advance system balance. [142]

I previously mentioned Coach Lasso. He is the fictional lead character in the show *Ted Lasso,* available on AppleTV. Ted, a small-time American football coach, is hired to coach a professional soccer team in England. The catch is that Ted has no experience coaching soccer. He receives a great deal of pushback from the players, the fans, and the locals. Watching Ted navigate the emotional turbulence of this new coaching gig with grace and skill is lovely.

Two moments in the first season are particularly significant, reflecting Ted's emotional balance. If you have watched the series, you know Ted's marriage is in trouble. His wife and son have remained in the United States but visit him in England. Near the end of the episode, right before Ted's wife and son climb into a cab to the airport, Ted has a poignant conversation with his wife, where he agrees to let her go. While he is sad about this choice, he realizes it is the best one for her and him. He also realizes that being in a relationship with someone who doesn't love him is not balanced for either person.

These realizations don't mean the choice doesn't hurt him, because it does. He just realizes letting go is best for both of them.

The second moment previously referenced is when Ted appropriately loses his temper at the team's star player, Jamie Tartt. Ted allows Jamie leeway to have his feelings and be a prima donna because Ted knows that there will be a perfect moment for engaging Jamie. And the system will let him know when that moment is. When that moment comes, Ted is ready. He expresses the right amount of frustration mixed with caring to make his stand. He carries a big stick that he can use anytime. But he doesn't. He waits for the moment to come to him and then swings for the fences and connects beautifully.

These four people are role models of Presenced Wholeness. They reveal how the human, divine, and navigator can come together to authentically express unique individuality from whole love. They exemplify balance.

Presenced Wholeness does not call us to be invasive or evasive. It calls us to stand in the middle of all that is happening in a moment and operate from the most balanced version of ourselves, in partnership with the universe. It's good to know what that looks like in the world because we don't often see it.

Allowing what is here and offering what is needed with whole love isn't the end. There are a few tasks left to do. After learning how to partner with the field of infinite possibilities, there is a natural emotional opening that invites curiosity about how big your balanced choices can be in service of making the world a more balanced system. I practiced choosing from a place of imbalance by trying to create the winning lottery ticket. Now it was time for me to practice choosing from balance.

The End of
Presenced Wholeness

At the beginning of this state, a person works on balancing humanity and divinity in the exercise of love. In the middle of this state, a person works on balancing humanity and divinity in the exercise of power. In the end, the time has come to embrace the infinite possibilities for your life from a place of balanced love and power. By this point, you've mastered balancing the nine indicators. Here, a person might ask this question: "What magically big things can I create that are aligned with the deepest parts of who I am and serve the greater good?" It's a beautiful question that allows you to explore emotional balance differently. While you are busy exploring, another emotional opening is materializing.

Maintaining your energy signature at 500 becomes second nature at this point. As previously explained at the end of Integration, at the frequency of 500 a person moves from experiencing insights to having revelations. Revelations restack the universe as a person recontextualizes the meaning of life events. A similar occurrence happens in this location as we move from the is-ness at the end of Silence & Oneness back into revelations across this state. As a reminder, revelations are dramatic disclosures about how we see the world, revealing our distorted perspective about life.

The revelations at the end of Presenced Wholeness relate to the upward arrow in the center of EI$^{3.0}$. The spiral in the center of the system that wraps around the arrow represents what is happening on the surface as one disentangles from the adapted identity. The center arrow represents what is occurring below the surface as one matures toward system balance as the loving creator. See Figure 2 in Chapter 1 for this arrow and spiral.

Like all emotional openings, we have to percolate in our experiences to see the deeper meaning. Here, I embodied emotional balance, which invited those deeper meanings to reveal themselves. I matured past seeing, knowing, and embodying emotional balance to reach what I affectionately termed the 34th level of *Jumanji*: system balance. System balance rests at the top of the arrow mentioned above. It is the systems perspective of balance for human endeavors, not just emotional balance. In system balance, we are and always have been a loving creator.

As I perched atop the spiral in the system I built, enjoying the fruits of my labor and feeling like I had conquered the world, the universe revealed that what I had built explained the surface dynamics of emotional balance. Not only was that revelation dramatic, it was also traumatic. The model reflects what we perceive happens to us as we develop emotional balance. Experiencing this dramatic disclosure felt like trying to discover a slow, hidden leak in a tire.

As I was finalizing the design of the ESI, I compared it to The Model of Emotional Development. Something didn't feel right. Whatever it was nagged at me. I kept comparing the two, looking for inconsistencies. What freed me to see that I had only captured the surface of balance development was this particular passage from *The Body Keeps Score: Brain, Mind, and Body in the Healing of Trauma* by Dr. Bessel Van Der Kolk:

> The lack of literature on the topic was a handicap, but my great teacher, Elvin Semrad, had taught us to be skeptical about textbooks. We had

only one real textbook, he said: our patients. We should trust only what we could learn from them—and from our own experience. This sounds so simple, but even as Semrad pushed us to rely upon self-knowledge, he also warned us how difficult that process really is, since human beings are experts in wishful thinking and obscuring the truth. I remember him saying: "The greatest sources of our suffering are the lies we tell ourselves." Working at the VA I soon discovered how excruciating it can be to face reality. This was truth both for my patients and for myself.[143]

After reading this passage, I repeatedly asked myself, "How is my understanding of emotional balance as presented wishful thinking, how does it obscure the truth, and what lies have I been telling myself?"

As I poked holes in my wishful thinking and my version of the truth, trying to resolve inconsistencies, I realized I was engaging in "balance" from the perspective of my imbalanced understanding of love and power. With all nine indicators in balance, I should have been maximizing the experience of balanced love and balanced power. However, I wasn't, and that was bothering me. That small leak ballooned into the realization that I didn't understand balance from the place of system balance and I didn't understand that I didn't understand that. As I ventured further down the rabbit hole of teasing out what balance looks like from a place of system balance, I began to feel ill. I had to put my work down and walk away. I would return, see more, write more, and get sick again. I dug deeper. I felt sick. I stopped. This pattern repeated itself for seven days as I reimagined my life, and all of life, through the lens of system balance.

What became evident is that we mistake our social engagement dynamics around control as love and power, which is why a balanced way of being with love and power is elusive. I thought I was in balance, but I wasn't. That was the reason I was struggling to maximize balanced love and balanced power. As we are taught these things, they don't exist. As children, almost all of us experienced social engagement dynamics that taught us to control and manipulate others using imbalanced notions of love and power, such as anger, compliance, resistance, helplessness, adoration, sex, and silence.

Since we do what we know, we have repeated those same dynamics in our adult lives, engaging in the same control and manipulation of others through anger, compliance, resistance, helplessness, adoration, sex, and silence. I have no judgment about these tactics or how you use them. I long used anger at being born sick as a primary method to get my way. I was damn good at it, too. I have used the other tactics as well. However, control is not love, nor is it power. While these tactics may allow us to conquer other people, they don't allow us to conquer ourselves or our biggest hopes and dreams.

The Model of Emotional Development is a map of what is happening superficially in our lives. It represents the imbalanced social engagement dynamics we engage in. You are not the dynamics you engage in. Separating yourself from those dynamics allows you to have more influence over them as you transform them toward balance. You are not unlovable. You are not powerless. You are not imbalanced. The dynamics of your social engagement with self, others, and the world are. That doesn't mean The Model of Emotional Development isn't helpful or is invalid. The model truly captures what we believe is happening to us in each state as it represents our perceptions. It can help you transform more efficiently and effectively.

This revelation invited me to recontextualize the meaning of my relationships across the arc of my life. Needless to say, I grieved the loss of my former way of life and spent some time crying over the many ways I had used the imbalanced social engagement dynamics of control as a substitute for love and power. As part of the recontextualizing, it became evident that system balance is about balanced engagement.

Life's journey is not to discover some unobtainable, nebulous ideal of enlightenment, or the balanced union of love and power, although that is what it feels like. Instead, it's a progression of moving toward a balanced being and doing. Thus, the end of Presenced Wholeness is about balanced engagement with the whole universe, not the use of balanced love and power. Balanced engagement is how system balance is brought to life.

The first part of the superficial, imbalanced social engagement dynamic is believing that love is a feeling. It's not. It is a way of being in the world where we allow all things to belong as they are with reverence for their essence. In this place of balanced being there is a resting of the controlling and manipulative tactics that we confuse for love. The greater process of the universe is not "Do no harm." Instead, it's "Allow everyone and everything to belong with reverence for who and what they are." In this place of balanced being, a person reveres all animate and inanimate objects simply because they exist. You embody love and that results in doing no harm.

A reason people who mature to Silence & Oneness choose to stay there is because the way of being love in that location is compelling and profound. It is likely the first time a person experiences love in its pure form as a way of being, not as an imbalanced social engagement dynamic.

The second part of the superficial, imbalanced social engagement dynamic is believing that power is about being right or getting your way. It's not. It's about choosing to create from your unique individuality in partnership with infinity to allow what is here and offer what is needed. In this place of balanced doing there is a resting of the controlling and manipulative tactics that we confuse for power. It's about creating:

- A self we love.
- A life we love.
- Using those creations to make the world a better place.

Because there is no resistance to the way life is, you presence your individuality in each moment to allow what is here and offer what is needed. You embody creation.

In balanced being, we are able to access balanced doing in a way that cannot be seen or understood from any other location in emotional development. In presencing our wholeness, we align with all of the universe through balanced engagement. "When your intention is unified in serving the greatest number of hearts and minds, the power of the universe is behind you."[144] You truly are a magical, creative ball of energy with unlimited possibilities in this location. You are love and you are creation, advocating for system balance from your true nature as the loving creator. More is offered on balanced engagement in Chapter 13.

What surprised me the most about this state was the occasional desire to disappear into infinity and relinquish my earthly suit. These feelings are not the same as suicidal thoughts. I don't think about my dissolution because life is horrible or because I think the world would be better off without me. There isn't a woundedness in these thoughts. They are more about being in relationship with the universe, myself, and infinity through creation. I allow these moments and feel whatever arises within. Then I remind myself that life is a damn good adventure. I choose to be part of the adventure for as long as possible to share EI$^{3.0}$ with as many people as possible. So I can advocate for system balance. So I can cry at as many Hallmark movies as possible with my husband. So I can laugh until I cry at the antics of my two sons. So I can meet my grandchildren. The human Tomi knows these experiences are not to be missed.

Remember, the patterns of less mature, emotional states are always available to us, whether good or bad. Think of the power of hubristic pride. Think of the power of the loss cycle. When we gather with other people, it is easy to get swept up in the moment and allow our behavior to drop to the lowest common denominator in the room. That statement is not an indictment of other people. It is a mere observation of the ways of humans, including people in Presenced Wholeness. It's also an acknowledgment of how powerful our human ways are.

Achieving Presenced Wholeness doesn't mean the journey is over. Heck, this is when the real fun begins. You get to be a magical, creative ball of energy until your human suit expires. What a lovely thought. And by the way, I am patiently waiting in the field of infinite possibilities for you to "Show me your magic!" It will be a joy for you to offer that same invitation to your clients.

TOMI'S TAKEAWAYS from This Chapter

- Your destiny is fulfilled in Presenced Wholeness.

- The gift of this state is emotional balance, where the use of love and power doesn't create new symptoms in the system.

- The work of being an advocate for system balance requires balanced engagement with all of life.

- As you embody love and creation, you can touch infinity and create from that place repeatedly as you allow what is here and offer what is needed.

- Less than half of 1 percent of the world's population is in Presenced Wholeness. Thus, the limitation is that you are likely creating, maintaining, and advancing system balance alone.

- The lower-vibrating human behaviors are always accessible.

- Table 6 maps the organic development path of the nine indicators in Presenced Wholeness and identifies the emotional openings that can occur here.

Chapter Twelve

THE TIMELINE FOR ACHIEVING BALANCE

As you think about your journey, or your client's journey, to system balance through these creation cycles of the emotional states, you should know there is no set timeline for how long it takes to discover your true nature as the loving creator. It takes as long as it takes for a person to mature to Presenced Wholeness (if that is the ultimate goal). For someone who adores efficiency and effectiveness, as I do, this might be the most challenging idea to accept.

Contemporary spiritual healer Thomas Hübl offered the best description I have heard of the journey of personal development. According to Hübl, part of our work as humans is to reclaim our natural state, to return to the unfragmented state where the soul can access the expansiveness and spaciousness of all that we are.[145] When the call to walk the path of personal transformation is heard and acted upon, you accept the lifelong task of doing the work. Experienced practitioners in the art of personal transformation know the arc of that journey spans from birth to death. These pearls of wisdom accompany this knowing:

- If I know that I am walking the path of personal transformation forever, I have time for now.[146]
- It's not about how long the journey takes; it's more about taking one step at a time.
- Experienced practitioners don't ask how long it is going to take, because it takes as long as it takes. Just walk.

If you accept that achieving system balance takes as long as it takes, you can shift your attention to the more important questions of "How much of an adventure will this be?" and "How do I make this my best year yet?" And doesn't that just fly in the face of my personal need to be efficient and effective? Of course it does, and that is the beauty of the journey. You learn to use your refined emotional imprints to impact what you know you can shift, and leave the rest for the universe to lead the way. Do the human things; do the divine things; and leave the rest to the gods.

The bottom line is that the length of the journey will mostly depend on you. Your ability to remain open and curious about the adventure will determine the pace of your progress. I encourage you to be curious about what your next step might be. Be curious about what you might not be seeing that needs to be seen. I invite you to use one of my favorite lines when you feel stuck or lost. Say to the universe or to the god of your religion, "Show me what needs to be seen.

I am open to the lesson." If you are open to the lesson on an expedited timeline, then the next chapter shares the liberating structures that reveal some shortcuts on the path to system balance.

TOMI'S TAKEAWAYS from This Chapter

- Allow the journey to unfold while you enjoy the adventure of it.
- Do the human things; do the divine things; and leave the rest to the gods.

Section IV

NEXT STEPS

Chapter Thirteen

LIBERATING STRUCTURES

D r. Hollis offers these words of wisdom on how the world could be different:

How different the world would be if each parent could say to the child: "Who you are is terrific, all you are meant to be. And who you are, as you are, is loved by all of us. You have a source within, which is the soul, and it will express itself to you through what we call desire. Always respect the well-being of the other, but live your own journey, serve that desire, risk being that which wishes to enter the world through you, and you will always have our love, even if your path takes you away from us." Such persons would then have a powerful tool to enable them to change their lives when it was not working out for them. Such persons would be able to make difficult decisions, mindful always of the impact on others, but also determined to live the life intended by the gods who brought us here.[147]

My parents didn't offer this message to me. They didn't know how. Your parents probably didn't do so, either. So how do you live the life intended by the gods who brought you here? How do you help your clients do that? I suggest that you do it by finding your way to emotional balance. Then you can help others in whatever way aligns with your unique individuality.

To live the life intended by the gods, balanced engagement is the more efficient and effective path. You must make the first move, though. No one can do the work for you. American self-help and spiritual author Dr. Wayne Dyer offered this advice: "The single most important tool to being in balance is knowing that you and you alone are responsible for the imbalance between what your dream life is meant to be, and the daily habits that drain life from that dream."[148] You can be presented with all the liberating structures in the world. None of them will matter if you aren't curious about how to move toward your best self.

Even when you recognize emotional openings for what they are, they don't come with a set of instructions. While it might be nice to know that on the twelfth day of being in Expression, at exactly the stroke of midnight, you execute steps A, B, and C, it doesn't work that way. At least not yet. However, suppose you are armed with a process that frees the power of the dynamics happening across a particular state. In that case, you can leverage those dynamics to evolve toward system balance without waiting for a defining moment to occur. Leveraging those dynamics is the objective of a liberating structure.

If you are already in the state of Presenced Wholeness, that is lovely. Please keep making bigger and bigger choices in service of the greater good and for your enjoyment. It is equally important to invite others to play in that space with you through your coaching practice. Suppose you are in some other emotional state and desire to evolve. In that case, you may not know how to take advantage of the emotional openings that occur on the journey to emotional balance. You may find it helpful to have more detail on the liberating structures available to you.

In this chapter, I provide an overview of the liberating structures I discovered that you can use for yourself or your clients to mature various indicators at the right time to expand the *comfort zone*. I think one of the most valuable aspects of these liberating structures, and a beautiful one as well, is that they don't usually threaten homeostasis. That means you can use them without activating the boundaries of the *comfort zone*.

I do not provide detail for every tool or task included in a liberating structure except for liberating structures for children. Instead, I name frameworks or tools I discovered or created that liberate the energy of the dynamics in a particular state. If you want to know more about the liberating structures mentioned in this chapter, then visit tomibryan.com for additional detail.

Balanced Engagement

Many coaching plans and treatment modalities don't yield outcomes we or our clients seek. We typically try to solve the challenge or fix the problem from our imbalanced location in The Model of Emotional Development. For most of us, that location represents an entanglement in the perspective that our self-image suffered harm that must be healed. Our self was never wounded nor distorted. We have always been and will always be loving creators.

Understanding that it is the dynamics of social engagement with self, others, and the world that are imbalanced clarifies next steps in a simple and uncomplicated way. A core methodology of balanced engagement is to allow everything as it is so its wisdom can be incorporated into the transformation process. Balanced engagement doesn't seek to fix anyone: no one is broken, and nothing is wrong with you or your client. The Paradoxical Theory of Change holds that change occurs when you become who you are, rather than when you try to become who you're not. Thus, the unlocking move isn't toward what you think you should be; it is toward what you already are. The focus of the liberating structures of $EI^{3.0}$ is to develop the capacities of balanced engagement by deepening into your unique personality and creating from that magical place.

Knowing that The Model of Emotional Development represents what is occurring on the surface of emotional development doesn't nullify its value as a transformational system. As a coach, if you want to help your clients realize as much of their potential as possible, you have to understand their experience so you can meet them where they are. The model allows you to see and appreciate exactly how the journey unfolds. However, to be as effective as possible, it is important to appreciate what is happening below the surface, so you can leverage those dynamics for faster transformation. Thus, liberating structures should focus on facilitating balanced engagement with the self, others, and the universe.

With a clear view of the dynamics taking place below the surface of emotional balance, it was simple to remove the background noise from the journey of balanced engagement. Here is the clear path:

1. Engage in activities that facilitate turning down the volume on anger, so space is created to see something new.
2. Develop skills that facilitate transformation out of The Drama Triangle.
3. Discover the unique personality and its special use.
4. Create from the unique personality by aiming the energy of it in a specific direction.
5. Open the heart.
6. Develop skills that facilitate transformation out of the *Life's fair* lifeview.
7. Partner with infinity to create for the greater good.
8. Develop the art of the balanced exchange with others through communication.
9. Learn and understand how to apply the greater processes of the universe.

Following this path allows alignment with the self from a place of balance, with others from a place of balance, and with infinity to create from a place of balance. Effortless joy, unlimited abundance, and good health are the norms here.

The first step on the way to balanced engagement is to take the ESI. The ESI reveals how a person sees themselves, identifying where that self-image locates them on the path of emotional development. When the coach knows the location, they see the *comfort zone* and the imbalanced dynamics the client is engaging in or that might greet the client upon taking the next step from the client's perspective. It allows the coach to meet the client where they are and speak their language so the client can hear the guidance offered. It has a two-way mirror effect. You see the client where they think they are on the development path of emotional balance, and you see where they really are on the development path of system balance.

The ESI informs the next step and includes using a liberating structure in the form of various tools that incrementally free the loving creator within, without activating the boundaries of the *comfort zone*. Once the location is known, leverage the appropriate tool or tools from this list to grow the skills of balanced engagement:

1. The Making Space Activity: this activity offers several methods for turning down the volume on anger. It is different from spewing because we aren't releasing to reinforce the feelings. We are releasing to make space for something new. This activity is recommended for clients in Protection.

2. The Greatness Guide: this guide offers activities for self-reflection, conversation, and skill development for transcending The Drama Triangle roles. This guide is recommended for clients in Protection.

3. The Balanced Exchange: this tool is one of those greater processes of the universe that offers some of the most effective communication tools for developing the balanced exchange with others. Some of the tools are recommended for clients at the end of Protection. Introduce advanced tools as the client matures.

4. The Talent DNA Worksheet: this worksheet facilitates discovering the facets of your unique personality that create

your talent DNA. Recommended for clients at the end of Protection. It is most useful in Expression.

5. The Purpose Worksheet: this worksheet facilitates discovering the particular use for your talent DNA. It is recommended for clients in Expression.

6. The Alignment Process: this process offers a way to aim the energy of your unique personality in a specific direction to create momentum. This process is recommended for clients in Expression.

7. The Open Heart Process: this process offers an integration method for transforming the emotional scrapheap. This process is recommended for clients at the end of Integration.

8. The Grounding Process: this tool is one of those greater processes of the universe that provides a method for grounding yourself in balance and leveraging creation. This process is recommended for clients in Presenced Wholeness.

These tools are designed to develop a person in tandem with the naturally occurring dynamics in each state. Following the path to balanced engagement and using the tools that free the loving creator within also provides the answers to these three existential questions: Who am I? Why am I here? What difference will I make?

While I recommend using specific tools at certain points in development, I lay out the whole path from beginning to end at the first meeting with a client. I like clients to know where they are going and exactly how they will get there.

If a person is in the beginning or middle of Protection, starting with The Making Space Activity is ideal. If you are a coach who has a client in Protection, keep chipping away at the anger using tools that allow the client to explore anger and its actions safely. It might not feel like you are making progress, and then one day, your client will surprise you in what they see about their actions. The same is true for yourself.

Additionally, take special care if the opening in Protection is a forceful defining moment like an arrest, an intervention, or the seeking of a safer space away from the abuse that has implications to well-being. In that case, the most crucial thing to do is immediately obtain the appropriate care necessary to restore or maintain well-being. If the defining moment has legal ramifications, hire qualified legal counsel to assist with the situation.

Because the fight mechanism is easily provoked in this state, to help a person evolve, we sometimes must wait for a person to reach constructive anger and its call of "what can be done about this?" Until people think something can be done about their circumstances, they will resign themselves to repeating the experience, yet expect different results. Once in constructive anger, the liberating structure is to brainstorm ways to answer the invitation to do something different and then take action.

Continue to remind yourself or those entrusted to your professional care that the next step a person takes is always their choice. Whatever action a client takes belongs to them and no one else.

Often, the best action to take for someone in Protection is to love them. And sometimes, loving them from afar is the best you can do as a coach. It is not your responsibility to fix others; they have to do that themselves. You can build the bridge, but they have to walk across it. When clients praise me for changing their lives, I reply, "I may have provided tools and guidance, but you had to do the work." Some people are not emotionally aware enough to see the need for the work, much less engage in the work. Allow them to belong just as they are and be there for them when ready.

If Protection is your starting point, and you aren't ready for a shift, then love yourself as you would your client and forgive yourself for not being in a place to grow. Determine that you will notice anger and its actions when you are ready. Then make the appropriate choice for yourself when the time comes.

If your goal is to remain in Silence & Oneness for the rest of your human days, liberating structures are not required. In this state, everything is complete, perfect, or just is. No action is required on your part to change anything. There is, however, a natural unfolding and deepening that happens here. Awareness, fully matured to embodiment, guides you as needed.

Many beautiful halo effects result from walking the path of balanced engagement. As your client builds new capacities and capabilities, they automatically extend those to others. For example, we don't need to learn to value others. As we learn to value ourselves and see our worth, we naturally value others. You can offer what you have, and give to yourself, to the world. The journey itself reveals how to be love and create from your unique personality in bigger, more magnanimous ways.

We can be more effective with our clients when we aren't standing in the illusion with them. Standing outside of the illusion will allow you to meet people where they are and hold the vision of the bigger picture for their life, while also knowing the dynamics at play below the surface of their sticking points. Understanding how the journey unfolds for the client and using language that speaks into the heart of what is happening for them makes them feel seen, heard, and loved. Feeling seen, heard, and loved in this way creates the container for unprecedented personal growth that might be elusive everywhere else in their life. You are also holding the space for balanced engagement to occur because you understand it is the greater objective, but your client can't see it yet. You don't view their bruised imprints as something to be refined, although that may be what you tell the client. You know the ultimate work is moving the imbalanced dynamics toward balance.

Balanced engagement is the way to discover your best self and have the most significant impact on others and the world. What greatness is your unique individuality the conduit for?

Liberating Structures for Children

Children are a special population that requires special attention—especially since youth is where we learn those imbalanced social engagement dynamics. If you are a parent, your instinct is to protect your child. Unfortunately, most of us weren't protected as children in ways that facilitated balanced engagement. As adults, we do what we know and what we know is what we learned from childhood. I reiterate, there is no judgment in that statement. It is just an observation about the system.

I put substantial effort into being a good parent, and I still feel like I failed in places. That is the nature of parenting. You aren't likely to give your children everything they need. As parents, we need to make peace with that and then do the best we can with what we have. To be a good parent to my two sons, I made up rules and games to help them grow in more balanced ways than I did. Because of the importance of raising emotionally balanced children, I not only name the structures here, I explain them, too:

- The hug rule
- The boundaries conversation
- The No Retribution game
- The 24-hour rule

The hug rule has long been one of my favorites. Actually, who I am kidding. They are all my favorites.

The hug rule is simple: Adults need nine hugs a day from their children to feel loved and safe. My children needed them, but I acted as if I needed them. The acting wasn't hard to do as I found great joy in those hugs. I still do.

The boundaries conversation is simple, too. It's your body, and you get to say who touches it and how. If someone tries to touch you without your permission, tell mom or dad. If it is a family member who is touching you inappropriately, tell a trusted adult at school. When it was age-appropriate, I introduced my children to values, and how to build boundaries around their values, so their life reflected what they deeply cared about.

The No Retribution game offered me deep belly laughs and a few gray hairs. One of my life goals is to have a strong family, one where we can say whatever needs to be communicated to each other from a place of deep caring for self and others. In order not to "shoot the messenger" with my children, I created a game called "No Retribution." The sole purpose of the No Retribution game was to create a space where it was safe to tell that something bad had happened and not get punished.

No Retribution started as a dinner-time game with my children. My husband and I mainly played it on Friday nights to engage our children in conversation about their week at school. Playing No Retribution involved a five-to-ten-minute period where all four of us took turns telling on ourselves about anything we had done during the week. The most important rule: there would be no punishment for what you did. Basically, we created a safe space to tattle on yourself, ease your conscience, and have no worries about punishment for the behavior. It made sharing dark secrets easier. It also seemed to make our transgressions less shameful, even if it was only in our heads.

My husband Jim's disclosures were always predictable: he ate somebody else's chocolate out of the freezer. My disclosures were usually pretty predictable, too: I drank a Pepsi I shouldn't have or ate more chocolate than I intended. When they were young, Shep and Warren's disclosures were fairly predictable as well. However, as they moved into their teens, Shep and Warren's disclosures became less predictable, and we stopped playing the game. Even though we stopped playing the game, Shep and Warren never stopped using the game. They just used it differently.

When one of the boys needed to share something they thought might upset us, they asked, "Can I have a no retribution moment?" When one of them said that to me, I knew I was about to hear something I probably didn't want to.

One morning I took one of the boys to breakfast (I am not going to divulge the name to protect the innocent and the guilty). While we were waiting for our food, this son looked me in the eye and said, "Can we have a no retribution moment?" I said sure. And then he let the story tumble out. What he had done violated just about every Bryan family value. It violated our family's vision of being effective people. It violated our family code (yes, we have a Bryan Family Code). His behavior made me angry. This child had done something to get himself thrown off my island. Yet, I had already promised no retribution! I could go on for days about my internal turmoil and internal discussion, but you get the picture.

Before I could respond, I had to take three deep gulps to compose myself. After I did that, I heard these words cross my lips: "And how did that work out for you?" Which led to a dialogue about why what my son had done wasn't wise, wasn't the best choice, and why he would likely not do that again. Thus, what started as a conversation that immediately created a few new gray hairs for me became one about my son evaluating his own behaviors and learning how to course correct them to be a more effective human being. I loved almost every second of it.

The 24-hour rule is about feeling what you feel when you feel it. For most of my life, I wasn't very adept at experiencing the experiences of my life. I didn't want that for my children. I wanted my two sons to feel life—whatever that looks like for them. In order to entice my sons to feel their feelings, I developed the 24-hour rule. When they got upset about something, I told them to wallow, cry, drink champagne or take tequila shots (when they were of age, of course), yell, beat their fists on their chests, or dance by the light of the moon. Do whatever they have to do to feel the feelings. Wallow in that righteous anger! Don't avoid it. Feel it. Celebrate that victory with a big smile or loud shouts of joy. However, when the 24 hours are up, they must leave the hurt, anger, joy, pride, or whatever in this moment, where it belongs, and take the wisdom of the moment forward.

Adults need this rule, too! Whatever the moment, remember that it is only one moment in a big life, so define it instead of letting it define you. The point of the 24-hour rule is to permit yourself to feel whatever it is you feel so no negative energy about the moment lingers. Doing so means it doesn't show up to haunt you later. We can mourn or celebrate long after the initial 24 hours. The point isn't to stop someone's grief or to cut short the joy. Each of us celebrates and grieves differently. I still miss my dad, who has been deceased for over two decades. When I experience potent moments of remembrance, they sadden me greatly and usually leave me in a puddle of tears. These feelings are important and meaningful. It means I cared. It means I loved deeply.

If we aren't trying to stop the grieving, what does the 24-hour rule do? It invites us to stop for 24 hours. To feel deeply. To stand in the middle of what is breaking our hearts, making us angry, disappointing us, frustrating us, or making us happy. To shut down, if that is what is needed. It makes it okay to stop, to experience the experience. It also teaches us that life goes on, and so must you. You don't have to quit grieving, crying, singing, celebrating, or whatever at 24 hours and one second. But you do have to get back up, brush yourself off, and march forward.

Finally, I recommend you print the words of Dr. Hollis that opened this chapter and place them on your refrigerator for all to see. While directed at your children, they are also valid for you.

At the end of the day, while these structures for children are important and should be used to teach children about balance, it is vital for you to move toward balance, too. It is challenging to be a model of balance for others when you aren't one for yourself. Your children will emulate what you model for them.

Chapter Fourteen

PRACTICE MAKES PERFECT

My bruises made for some great conversation, didn't they? I will always be a work in progress because of the deep emotional vat I percolated in as a child. My ongoing development means I continue to create, find, and use new liberating structures to support my climb out of the vat. Even though I profess to be in Presenced Wholeness, where I practice creating, maintaining, and advancing system balance and seeking to create bigger and bigger things in service of the greater good and for my enjoyment, I am first and foremost a human. As such, I will do the human things. System balance is an ongoing pursuit until the day I surrender my human suit.

Because system balance is required for sustaining your true nature as a loving creator, liberating structures aren't intended for one-time use. We must return to them repeatedly because balanced engagement "is an ongoing process, deepening the insights, discoveries and adjustments that we make."[149] Because practice makes perfect.

It took years for us to develop our bruised emotional imprints' patterns, ruts, and grooves. It is unlikely we will free ourselves from these patterns using a liberating structure once—although that is always my wish for you and for myself.

Knowing that those imprints can be powerful forces, here is how you best benefit from liberating structures:

> If this were a book about tennis, golf, or skiing, you would read it knowing that its value would come only when you have practiced the methods and learned from them. This is the secret of how to learn and benefit from Liberating Structures: just do it, plunge in, explore, and practice as often as possible, taking advantage of the opportunities that abound daily. Be assured that no matter which Liberating Structure you try, in whatever situation, you will generate surprisingly better results than expected.[150]

Practice as often as possible.

Dr. Remen summarized the value and importance of practice:

> I am always tuning my orchestra. Somewhere deep inside there is a sound that is mine alone, and I struggle daily to hear it and tune my life to it. Sometimes there are people and situations that help me to hear my note more clearly; other times people and situations make it harder for me to hear. A lot depends on my commitment to listening and my intention to stay coherent with this note. It is only when my life is tuned to my note that I can play life's mysterious and holy music without tainting it with my own bitterness, resentment, agendas, and fears.[151]

As you tune your life to your clear note, know that laughter and tears are some of the best medicines. "The more you can laugh at yourself, the easier the journey. Fortunately, there's no shortage of material."[152] Laugh your way through it or cry your way through it, as appropriate, and I promise all will be as it is supposed to be.

Remember, I created this book as a map of emotional balance and, ultimately, system balance. You can also use it to achieve balance if that is your wish. My words and descriptions may not align with what occurs precisely in each moment, because some of the events that take place across this journey defy words. Additionally, the timing of emotional openings might be slightly off in regard to whether something happens at the beginning, middle, or end of a particular emotional state. Each of us is a one-of-a-kind mosaic and that will make for different experiences. That said, I do believe what I have captured and offered in The Model of Emotional Development accurately describes the process; it just may not unfold in the exact order I have prescribed. Plus, this map isn't about perfection. It's about offering a way to initiate a deeper conversation on balance, and that will always be messy because life is messy. And isn't that beautiful?

Armed with the wisdom shared in this book, you now have a larger question to drive your curiosity. Howard Falco wrote, "The question is never one of *if you matter* as an individual experience of consciousness, but rather of *how you will CHOOSE to matter* in your world from this very moment onward."[153] I challenge you to consider how you will choose to matter from this very moment forward in a balanced way that brings you joy and serves the greater good.

As you take the first steps on the path of balance, I invite you to live in the present moment in partnership with infinity, instead of living in the present in partnership with the past. Choose to matter by discovering and embracing your true nature. Do the human things and the divine things. There is no greater human power or presence.

May this be your best year yet.

Acknowledgments

B ringing Emotional Intelligence 3.0 out of my head and into the world was not a one-woman show. First, I had to have the childhood experiences that shaped who I am. For that, I offer gratitude to my dad, Thomas White, my mom, Janie White, and my siblings, Jerry, Mike, and Janie. I then had to shift and grow. For that, I offer gratitude to my husband, Jim, my two sons, Shep and Warren, and their significant others, Caroline and Kayla, and my refining friends. Finally, I had to keep revising the model until it felt genuine. For that, I offer gratitude to Karen McClamrock, Daniel Morman, Susan Harding, Bunmi Collins, and Carolyn Leasure.

To everyone at Scribe, thank you for purifying the note this book plays in the symphony of the universe. It is now a sound lovelier than I could have imagined.

To Tom Suher, thank you for helping me honor the legal lines. I appreciate you and your mad legal skills.

Thank you to all the others I have crossed paths with, whether briefly or for an extended time, whether a positive experience or not.

You shaped some aspect of who I am and what I have created with my life. I honor you and convey my gratitude for your contributions to my journey of emotional balance.

Onward and upward,
Tomi

About the Author

Dr. Tomi White Bryan has long been fascinated with creating maps and tools that simplify the complexities of life. She has used these tools to become a lawyer, university professor, compliance and leadership consultant, executive coach, and senior leader in two global organizations. She has written four other self-help books, three of them under the pen name Tomi Llama.

An avid learner, she believes life is a grand adventure. When she isn't sitting on the back porch of her North Carolina home with her tennis-loving husband and tennis-ball-fetching black lab, she enjoys her latest career as a coach, keynote speaker, and facilitator. Connect with her at tomibryan.com.

Notes

Chapter One

[1] Patrick Monahan, Espen Lind, and Amund Bjørklund, "Bruises," recorded by Train featuring Ashley Monroe, *California 37*, 2012.

[2] Jack Zenger and Joseph Folkman, *The Extraordinary Leader: Turning Good Managers into Great Leaders* (New York, NY: McGraw-Hill, 2009), 149.

Chapter Two

[3] Zenger and Folkman, *The Extraordinary Leader*.

[4] Zenger and Folkman, *The Extraordinary Leader*; Joseph Folkman, "History Of 360s: Why We Moved From Focusing On Weaknesses To Strengths," *Forbes*, October 25, 2018, https://www.forbes.com/sites/joefolkman/2018/10/25/history-of-360s-why-we-moved-from-focusing-on-weaknesses-to-strengths/?sh=a4ab13dd77bc.

[5] Parker J. Palmer, "Living From the Inside Out," (commencement address, Naropa University, May 10, 2015), https://www.youtube.com/watch?v=MaOFkumhcCU.

[6] Jerry Colonna, *Reboot: Leadership And The Art Of Growing Up* (New York: HarperBusiness, 2019), 226.

7   Andrew Blundell, "Righteous Indignation—How Useful Is It, Really?" Harley Therapy Counseling Blog, June 18, 2020, https://www.harleytherapy.co.uk/counselling/righteous-indignation.htm.

8   Abhi Golhar, "10 Ways to Increase Your Emotional Intelligence: Developing your EQ skills is essential to professional success today." Inc. September 21 2018, https://www.inc.com/young-entrepreneur-council/10-ways-to-increase-your-emotional-intelligence.html.

9   Travis Bradberry, "Emotional Intelligence—EQ," *Forbes*, January 9, 2014, https://www.forbes.com/sites/travisbradberry/2014/01/09/emotional-intelligence/?sh=6df3ae831ac0.

10 David R. Hawkins, *Letting Go: The Pathway of Surrender* (Sedona, AZ: Veritas Publishing, 2012), 231-232.

11 Joseph Campbell, *A Joseph Campbell Collection: Reflections on the Art of Living*, electronic edition, edited by Robert Walter (Joseph Campbell Foundation: 2011), 16.

Chapter Three

12 David R. Hawkins, *Transcending the Levels of Consciousness: The Stairway to Enlightenment* (Carlsbad, CA: Hay House, 2006), 305.

13 Rachel Naomi Remen, *My Grandfather's Blessings: Stories of Strength, Refuge, and Belonging* (New York, NY: Penguin, 2001), 255.

14 Peter Senge et al., *The Fifth Discipline Fieldbook: Strategies and Tools for Building a Learning Organization* (New York, NY: Doubleday, 1994), 89.

15 Peter Senge, *The Fifth Discipline: The Art & Practice of The Learning Organization* (New York, NY: Currency, 1990), 69.

16 Senge et al., *The Fifth Discipline Fieldbook*, 90.

17 David Hawkins, *The Eye of the I: From Which Nothing is Hidden* (Carlsbad, CA: Hay House, 2001), 281.

18 Henri Lipmanowicz and Keith McCandless, *The Surprising Power of Liberating Structures: Simple Rules to Unleash A Culture of Innovation* (Liberating Structures Press, 2013), x.

19 Senge, *The Fifth Discipline*, 7.

20 Paul O., *You Can't Make Me Angry* (Torrance, CA: Capizon Publishing, 1999), 112.

Chapter Four

21 "FBI Whistleblower Wins Retaliation Claims," National Whistleblower Center, accessed March 9, 2022, https://www.whistleblowers.org/news/fbi-whistleblower-wins-retaliation-claims/.

22 Albion M. Butters, "A brief history of Spiral Dynamics," *Approaching Religion* vol. 5, no. 2 (November 2015): 68–69.

23 Butters, "A brief history of Spiral Dynamics," 69.

24 Butters, "A brief history of Spiral Dynamics," 69.

25 Greg McKeown, *Essentialism: The Disciplined Pursuit of Less* (New York, NY: Crown Publishing Group, 2014), 196.

26 Hawkins, *Transcending the Levels of Consciousness*, 311.

27 Anodea Judith and Lion Goodman, *Creating on Purpose: The Spiritual Technology of Manifesting Through the Chakras* (Boulder, CO: Sounds True, 2012), 28.

28 Attributed to Nikola Tesla in Ralph Bergstresser, "Comments from the Inventor of Purple Harmony Plates," accessed March 9, 2022, https://www.bibliotecapleyades.net/ciencia/esp_ciencia_universalenergy02.htm.

29 Arjun Walia, "Nothing Is Solid & Everything Is Energy—Scientists Explain The World of Quantum Physics," *Collective Evolution*, September 27, 2014, https://www.collective-evolution.com/2014/09/27/this-is-the-world-of-quantum-physics-nothing-is-solid-and-everything-is-energy/.

30 Derek Rydall, *Emergence: Seven Steps for Radical Life Change* (New York, NY: Atria Paperback, 2015), 33–34.

31 "The Law Of Resonance Provides The Answers As To How The Law Of Attraction Operates And How You Can Use It to Create More Desired Events, Conditions and Circumstances In Your Life," Abundance-And-Happiness. com, accessed March 9, 2022, http://www.abundance-and-happiness.com/law-of-resonance.html.

32 David R. Hawkins, *Power vs. Force: The Hidden Determinants of Human Behavior* (Carlsbad, CA: Hay House 1985), 68–69.

33 Hawkins, *Letting Go*, 32.

34 Hawkins, *Transcending the Levels of Consciousness*, 303.

35 Hawkins, *Power vs. Force*, 76.

36 Mike Dooley, *Infinite Possibilities: The Art of Living Your Dreams* (New York, NY: Atria Books), 41.

Chapter Five

37 James Hollis, *Hauntings: Dispelling the Ghosts Who Run Our Lives* (Asheville, NC: Chiron Publications, 2015), 5.

38 Hollis, *Hauntings*, 13.

39 Hollis, *Hauntings*, 13.

40 Jakob Robert Schneider, *Family Constellations: Basic Principles and Procedures* (Heidelberg: Carl-Auer, 2007), 34.

41 Tarra Bates-Duford, "Blind Family Loyalties: 7 Types," Psychcentral.com, August 10, 2017, https://psychcentral.com/blog/relationship-corner/2017/08/blind-family-loyalties-7-types#1.

42 Bates-Duford, "Blind Family Loyalties."

43 Bates-Duford, "Blind Family Loyalties."

44 Mario Martinez, *The MindBody Self: How Longevity Is Culturally Learned and the Causes of Health are Inherited* (Carlsbad, CA: Hay House, 2017), 1.

45 Carolyn Myss, *Invisible Acts of Power: Personal Choices That Create Miracles* (Boulder, CO: Sounds True, November 18, 2004), CD set.

46 Hawkins, *Letting Go*, 9.

47 Tara Bennett-Goleman, *Emotional Alchemy: How the Mind Can Heal the Heart* (New York, NY: Three Rivers Press, 2001), 87.

48 Margaret Paul, "What Are Emotional Triggers + Why You Need To Understand Them," Mind Body Green, updated February 24, 2020,

https://www.mindbodygreen.com/0-18348/what-are-emotional-triggers-why-you-need-to-understand-them.html.

49 Abigail Brenner, "5 Benefits of Stepping Outside Your Comfort Zone: Why moving beyond the safe and familiar is essential for growth," *Psychology Today*, December 27, 2015, https://www.psychologytoday.com/us/blog/in-flux/201512/5-benefits-stepping-outside-your-comfort-zone.

50 "Homesostasis," *Encyclopedia Britannica*, updated May 27, 2020, https://www.britannica.com/science/homeostasis.

51 Jayne Lenoard, "Cognitive Dissonance: What to know," Medical News Today, October 21, 2019, https://www.medicalnewstoday.com/articles/326738.

52 Howard Falco, *Time in a Bottle: Mastering the Experience of Life* (New York, NY: Jeremy P. Tarcher/Penguin, 2014), 76.

53 Gay Hendricks, *The Big Leap: Conquer Your Hidden Fear and Take Life to the Next Level* (New York, NY: HarperOne, 2009), 26.

54 Jennifer Warner, "Bad Memories Easier to Remember: Negative Memories May Be More Vivid Than Happy Ones," WebMD, August 29, 2007, https://www.webmd.com/brain/news/20070829/bad-memories-easier-to-remember.

55 Bennett-Goleman, *Emotional Alchemy*, 127-128.

56 Susan Campbell, *Getting Real: Ten Truth Skills You Need to Live an Authentic Life* (Novato, CA: HJ Kramer/New World Library, 2001), xvi.

57 Bennett-Goleman, *Emotional Alchemy*, 87.

Chapter Six

58 Jaya Jaya Myra, *Vibrational Healing: Attain Balance & Wholeness * Understand Your Energetic Type* (Woodbury, MN: Llewellyn Publications, 2015), 81.

59 Hawkins, *Power vs. Force*, 90-91.

60 "Anger," American Psychological Association, accessed March 9, 2022, https://www.apa.org/topics/anger.

61 David Emerald, *The Power of TED* (The Empowerment Dynamic)* (Bainbridge Island, WA: Polaris Publishing, 2016).

[62] Lynne Forrest with Eileen Meagher, *Beyond Victim Consciousness: Guiding Principles for Life* (Irvington, NY: Conscious Living Media, 2011).

[63] Stephen A. Diamond, "Essential Secrets of Psychotherapy: Fate, Destiny and Responsibility," *Psychology Today*, July 23, 2008, https://www.psychology today.com/au/blog/evil-deeds/200807/essential-secrets-psychotherapy-fate-destiny-and-responsibility?amp.

[64] Diamond, "Essential Secrets of Psychotherapy."

[65] Diamond, "Essential Secrets of Psychotherapy."

[66] Peter Michaelson, "The Invisible Wall of Psychological Resistance," WhyWe Suffer.com, December 5, 2016, https://whywesuffer.com/the-invisible-wall-of-psychological-resistance/.

[67] Falco, *Time in a Bottle*, 43.

[68] Michael Singer, *The Surrender Experiment: My Journey into Life's Perfection* (New York, NY: Harmony Books, 2015), 4.

[69] Arthur Schopenhauer, *Studies in Pessimism: A Series of Essays* (London: S. Sonnenschein & Company, 1981), 69.

[70] Diana Winston, "What is 'Natural Awareness'?" Ten Percent Happier, February 26, 2019, https://www.tenpercent.com/meditationweeklyblog/what-is-natural-awareness.

[71] Barbara Nordstrom-Loeb, "Embodiment—How to get it and why it is important," University of Minnesota Center for Spirituality & Healing, February 12, 2018, https://www.csh.umn.edu/news-events/blog/thoughts-about-embodiment-how-get-it-and-why-it-important.

[72] Otto C. Scharmer, *Theory U: Leading from the Future as It Emerges* (San Francisco, CA: Berrett-Kohler Publishers, Inc., 2009), xiv.

[73] Celeste Kidd and Benjamin Y. Haden, "The Psychology and Neuroscience of Curiosity." *Neuron* vol. 88 (November 4, 2015): 449.

[74] Kidd and Haden, "The Psychology and Neuroscience of Curiosity," 450.

[75] Kidd and Haden, "The Psychology and Neuroscience of Curiosity," 451.

[76] Peter Block, *Community: The Structure of Belonging* (San Francisco, CA: Berrett-Kohler Publishers, Inc., 2018), 107.

[77] Block, *Community*, 107.

[78] Eugène Ionesco, *Découvertes* (Paris: Albert Skira, 1969), as quoted by Stuart Wells, *Choosing the Future: The Power of Strategic Thinking* (New York: Butterworth-Heinemann, 1997), 15.

[79] Kidd and Haden, "The Psychology and Neuroscience of Curiosity," 451.

[80] Alex Shashkevich, "The power of language: how words shape people, culture," *Stanford News* online, August 22, 2019, https://news.stanford.edu/2019/08/22/the-power-of-language-how-words-shape-people-culture/.

[81] Shashkevich, "The power of language."

[82] Dave Logan, John King, and Halee Fischer-Wright, *Tribal Leadership: Leveraging Natural Groups to Build a Thriving Organization* (New York, NY: HarperCollins, 2008), 28.

[83] Logan, King, and Fischer-Wright, *Tribal Leadership*, 10.

[84] David Logan, Tribal Leadership (TED-Ed lecture, July 17, 2013), https://www.youtube.com/watch?v=ATbyOuk0bvE; Logan, King, and Fischer-Wright, *Tribal Leadership*, 25.

[85] Logan, King, and Fischer-Wright, *Tribal Leadership*, 29.

[86] Logan, *Tribal Leadership* (lecture).

[87] David Kessler, *Finding Meaning: The SIXTH STAGE of GRIEF* (New York, NY: Scribner, 2019), 1-2.

[88] Travis Bradberry and Jean Greaves, *Emotional Intelligence 2.0* (San Diego, CA: TalentSmart, 2009), 55.

Chapter Seven

[89] Jim Dethmer, "Having and Being Enough" (lecture, Coaching From Source, online, October 4, 2018). Dethmer noted that his work was adopted from the work of Michael Bernard Beckwith.

[90] Hawkins, *Letting Go*, 9.

[91] Hawkins, *Letting Go*, 12.

[92] Bradberry and Greaves, *Emotional Intelligence 2.0*, 13.

[93] Victoria Castle, *The Trance of Scarcity: Stop Holding Your Breath and Start Living Your Life* (Oakland, CA: Berrett-Koehler Publishers, 2007), 25.

[94] Logan, King, and Fischer-Wright, *Tribal Leadership*, 18.

[95] Logan, King, and Fischer-Wright, *Tribal Leadership*, 45.

[96] Singer, *The Surrender Experiment*, 7.

[97] J.C. Maxwell, *Leadership Gold* (Nashville, TN: Thomas Nelson, 2008), 22–23.

[98] Kessler, *Finding Meaning*, 3.

[99] Logan, King, and Fischer-Wright, *Tribal Leadership*, 52.

[100] Logan, King, and Fischer-Wright, *Tribal Leadership*, 19.

[101] O, *You Can't Make Me Angry*, 116.

[102] Charles Carver and Sheri Johnson, "Authentic and Hubristic Pride: Differential Relations to Aspects of Goal Regulation, Affect, and Self-Control." *Journal of Research in Personality* vol. 44, no. 6. (December 2011), https://www.ncbi.nlm.nih.gov/pmc/articles/PMC3137237/.

[103] Jessica Tracy, "The 'Deadly Sin': The Positive and Negative Power of Pride," (interview by Knowledge@Wharton staff, November 2, 2016).

[104] Paula Cocozza, "A new start after 60: 'I was sick, tired and had lost myself—until I began lifting weights at 71," *The Guardian*, July 23, 2021, https://www.theguardian.com/lifeandstyle/2021/jul/23/a-new-start-after-60-i-was-sick-tired-and-had-lost-myself-until-i-took-up-bodybuilding-at-71.

[105] Cocozza, "A new start after 60."

[106] Cocozza, "A new start after 60."

Chapter Eight

[107] Dethmer, "Having and Being Enough."

[108] Blundell, "Righteous Indignation—How Useful Is It, Really?"

[109] Leon Seltzer, "The Rarely Recognized Upside of Anger," *Psychology Today*, May 6, 2014, https://www.psychologytoday.com/us/blog/evolution-the-self/201405/the-rarely-recognized-upside-anger.

Chapter Nine

[110] Dethmer, "Having and Being Enough."

[111] Michael Brown, *The Presence Process: A Healing Journey into Present Moment Awareness* (Vancouver, British Columbia: Namaste Books, 2018), 277.

[112] Steven R. Covey, *The 7 Habits of Highly Effective People: Powerful Lessons in Personal Change*, 30th Anniversary Edition (New York: Simon & Schuster, 2020), 209.

[113] Marc Brackett, *Permission to Feel: The Power of Emotional Intelligence to Achieve Well-being and Success* (New York, NY: Celadon Books, 2019), 13.

[114] Deborah MacNamara, "Softening the Hardened Heart," Neufeld Institute, https://neufeldinstitute.org/softening-the-hardened-heart.

[115] Lior Arussy, *Next is Now: 5 Steps for Embracing Change* (New York, NY: Simon & Schuster, 2018), 108.

[116] O., *You Can't Make Me Angry*, 61.

[117] Falco, *Time in a Bottle*, 90.

[118] Dethmer, "Having and Being Enough."

[119] Pema Chodron, *Taking the Leap: Freeing Ourselves from Old Habits and Fears* (Boulder, CO: Shambhala Publications, 2019), 36.

[120] Chodron, *Taking the Leap.*, 37.

[121] "What Is Forgiveness?" *Greater Good Magazine*, accessed March 9, 2022, https://greatergood.berkeley.edu/topic/forgiveness/definition.

[122] Burke Miller, *A Sacred Trust: The Four Disciplines of Conscious Leadership* (Boulder, CO: White Wolf Wisdom Press, 2019), 150.

[123] Hawkins, *Transcending the Levels of Consciousness*, 317.

Chapter Ten

[124] Hawkins, *Letting Go*, 182.

[125] Michael Roach, *The Diamond Cutter: The Buddha on Managing Your Business and Your Life* (New York, NY: Doubleday, 2009), 216.

[126] Hawkins, *Transcending the Levels of Consciousness*, 242.

[127] Harold Becker, "Unconditional Love," The Love Foundation, accessed March 9, 2022, http://www.thelovefoundation.com/whoweare/unconditionallove.html.

[128] Hawkins, *Letting Go*, 178.

[129] Hawkins, *Power vs. Force*, 91–92.

[130] Hawkins, *Letting Go*, 182.

[131] Walt Whitman, "Song of Myself," in *Leaves of Grass*, section 51.

Chapter Eleven

[132] Robert Ohotto, *Transforming Fate into Destiny: A New Dialogue with Your Soul* (Carlsbad, CA: Hay House, 2008), xxxi.

[133] Ohotto, *Transforming Fate into Destiny*, 4.

[134] Mario Martinez, *The MindBody Code: How to Change the Beliefs that Limit Your Health, Longevity, and Success* (Boulder, CO: Sounds True, 2014), CD set.

[135] Myra, *Vibrational Healing*, 81.

[136] Hawkins, *Power vs Force*, 91–92.

[137] Ruth King, "How to Be Equanimous in a Racialized World," December 21, 2018, https://www.lionsroar.com/how-to-be-equanimous-in-a-racialized-world/.

[138] Singer, *The Surrender Experiment*, 65.

[139] Singer, *The Surrender Experiment*, 77.

[140] "Principle Commitments," His Holiness the 14th Dalai Lama, accessed March 9, 2022, https://www.dalailama.com/the-dalai-lama/biography-and-daily-life/three-main-commitments.

[141] "Our Mission," Obama Foundation, accessed April 13, 2022, https://www.obama.org/mission/.

[142] "Our Mission," The Carter Center, accessed April 13, 2022, https://www.carter center.org/about/mission.html.

[143] Bessel van der Kolk, *The Body Keeps the Score: Brain, Mind, and Body in the Healing of Trauma* (New York: New York, Penguin Books, 2015), 11.

[144] Falco, *Time in a Bottle*, 90.

Chapter Twelve

[145] Thomas Hübl, "Conscious Healing Session 1" (lecture, online, December 1, 2019).

[146] Hübl, "Conscious Healing Session."

Chapter Thirteen

[147] Hollis, *Hauntings*, 129.

[148] Wayne Dyer, *Being in Balance* (Hay House, Inc.: 2016), excerpted as "How to Create Life Balance Between Dreams and Habits," *Wayne's Blog*, accessed March 9, 2022, https://www.drwaynedyer.com/blog/create-balance-dreams-habits/.

Chapter Fourteen

[149] Bennett-Goleman, *Emotional Alchemy*, 301.

[150] Lipmanowicz and McCandless, *The Surprising Power of Liberating Structures*, xi.

[151] Remen, *My Grandfather's Blessings*, 49.

[152] Castle, *The Trance of Scarcity*, 46.

[153] Falco, *Time in a Bottle*, 179.